Discard

# altered
## CLOTHING

To Donald Brooks, whose work inspired my designs for this book

First published in the United States of America by
Quarry Books, a member of
Quayside Publishing Group
33 Commercial Street
Gloucester, Massachusetts 01930-5089
Telephone: (978) 282-9590
Fax: (978) 283-2742
www.rockpub.com

**Library of Congress Cataloging-in-Publication Data**
Maggio, Kathleen
   Altered clothing : hip fixes and transformations with a needle and
thread / Kathleen Maggio and Timothy Maggio.
      p.    cm.—(Domestic arts for crafty girls)
   ISBN 1-59253-246-2 (pbk.)
   1. Clothing and dress—Alteration. 2. Clothing and dress—
Remaking. I. Maggio, Timothy. II. Title. III. Series.
   TT550.M24 2006
   646.4'04—dc22                                2006008906
                                                CIP
ISBN-13: 978-1-59253-246-9
ISBN-10: 1-59253-246-2

10  9  8  7  6  5  4  3  2  1
Cover and Book Design: Rockport Publishers
Cover Image and Photography: Timothy Maggio of Vinepod, Inc.
Photographs on pages 8–11 courtesy of www.istock.com
Technical Editor: Susan Huxley
Assistant Technical Editor: Katherine Riess

Printed in Singapore

# altered
## CLOTHING

hip fixes and
transformations
with a needle
and thread

**KATHLEEN MAGGIO**
**PHOTOGRAPHY BY TIMOTHY MAGGIO**

✳ domestic arts for crafty girls

GLOUCESTER MASSACHUSETTS

QUARRY BOOKS

contents

introduction

**The term "alterations" invokes images** of artful tailors, with pins between their lips, turning up a hem. Sadly, this is becoming a lost art. Contributing to this is the wide selection of clothing that is inexpensive and readily accessible.

Over the past few decades, many of us have become too busy to spend time on our wardrobes. However, custom pieces made from ready-made clothes can be completed in an afternoon. Transforming an existing garment is a satisfying and economically sound alternative to purchasing new clothes each season. And that transformation is what this book is all about.

This is not a book about fitting. While it does address some basic alteration techniques such as hemming, this book shows you how cutting, stitching, and ornamentation can make over a garment into something new and exciting. By adding details, color, and texture, your clothes will reflect your personality and style.

Everyone wants to look unique. We want to wear things that we can relate to and experiment with. We want to stand apart from the crowd. I wore a uniform my first eight years in school. By the time I entered public high school, I was desperate to express my individual fashion sense. Most evenings were spent sewing something new to wear the next day.

Recycling clothes makes perfect sense in today's environment. I value clothing whether it was a gift or something I used precious time to purchase or make. There is a skirt in my closet that I made fifteen years ago. It has undergone three face-lifts and it still looks great. I do occasionally drop off donations at secondhand stores, but if there is a way to redo a favorite but outdated sweater, that is when I apply a little ingenuity.

It has become fashionable to shop at thrift stores given the variety and savings. Many of us feel there are more important things to spend our money on than overpriced, mass-produced clothing. Certainly, some vintage clothes are of extraordinary quality and detail, unmatched in today's market. As the saying goes, "They don't make 'em like they used to." Usually, these garments are only in need of a belt, buttons, or other small details. These minor additions can provide a whole new look.

We all know what we want in our clothes. Some want to make a quiet statement, while others convey loud messages about their personality. One of my students came to class wearing a sheer appliquéd piece that was tied above the bust over layered T-shirts. She said it was a vintage apron, and wore it as an overskirt one day and a top the next.

Fashion moves fast and is constantly changing. With the techniques you will learn in this book, you can translate a look seen on the street today into a garment you can wear tomorrow! All you need are some basic sewing skills and a keen eye for trends. Make a statement and reference your own history, ethnicity, and lifestyle.

Making and refashioning clothes is highly creative and empowering. I am happy to have this opportunity to share my ideas with you.

# getting started

## BEGIN WITH

a garment and an idea for restyling it. A **skirt** or **T-shirt** is a great place to start. If you are considering using an **embellishment**, take a look at the Trims list that follows to think about the possibilities. Tools will be needed to implement your alteration. Refer to Techniques on page 20 for sewing information.

1

# clothes and inspiration

**At the back of your closet** or the bottom of your dresser drawer there are probably clothes in need of updating. Try them on in front of a mirror and assess whether they have make-over potential. Menswear, hats, shoes, bags, and belts are also full of possibilities.

Looking for something to work on that's got some history? It can be found at a thrift store or antique shop (and don't forget Grandma's attic). Be careful to select clothes that are in good condition. The quality of the fabric and fit are important. Stained and torn pieces can be a problem unless your plans include patches or some other type of camouflage like dyeing the fabric. Clothes more than forty years old are fragile and must be handled with extra care.

Read garment labels for fabric content and cleaning instructions. If these are missing, judge by the feel and drape of the fabric. Hand washables can be washed before the alteration process. Since the cost of dry cleaning exceeds the cost of a thrift store item, wait and have it cleaned after the alteration is done and you are pleased with the results.

In most cases, the garment itself will inspire its transformation. Each season, garment proportions change in length and width. For example, when low waistlines are the rage, an alteration could involve removing the waistband and replacing it with a facing. Shortening a hemline is easy; lengthening it requires extra fabric or trim. Structural alterations involve removing the sleeves and taking the garment in at the side seams. Changes range from replacing the buttons and belt to transforming the garment's function.

Fashion magazines and newspapers are a great resource for current trends and ideas. Create a file of fashion clippings. A three-ring binder filled with sheet protectors will hold tear sheets of your favorite looks. Reference costume history books for design inspiration.

# trims

**Decorative treasures** can sometimes be found in an inherited box of buttons or lace. Fabric scraps, scarves, embroidered curtains, and tablecloths are trim possibilities, as well. Parts of one garment can serve to adorn another. Let the fabric of your garment speak to you.

## beads and sequins

Decorative beads come in all shapes and sizes. If applying them individually, use beading needles because the holes are small. Sequins have a center hole and lay flat on the fabric. Paillettes are larger disks similar to sequins that have a hole close to the edge so they hang.

## belts

Any material may be used for belts as long as it is interfaced or backed. Felt, ribbons, and leather are good candidates since they don't fray.

## buckles

D-rings, clasps, and buckles without prongs are easy to use when creating belts. The width of the original belt will be apparent by the existing belt loops. If there are none, obtain the buckle first, then make the belt based on the width of the buckle. Covered buckle kits are also available.

## buttons

When selecting button replacements, test the new button by putting it through an existing buttonhole. Flat and shank buttons generally correspond to the fabric thickness. Customize buttons by covering them with contrasting fabric. Use a covered button kit.

## cords

Cable cord is white twisted cotton, available in different thicknesses. It's used for drawstrings, piping, and topical decoration and can be dyed any color. There are many other types of cord used for tying and trim. Soutache braid is flat and can be stitched to fabric like cord.

## eyelets and grommets

An eyelet is a small hole made for receiving a cord, hook, or belt buckle prong. It can be embroidered or a metal ring set in the fabric. Eyelets, grommets, and gripper snaps are both functional and decorative. The metal type are applied with special pliers or a setter and hammer.

## feathers and fur

Feathers are usually glued individually onto accessories and fabric. The quills are then covered with a beaded appliqué or bow. Feather boas are attached with a needle and thread. Fur pieces can be stitched to a detachable collar, pocket edge, or hem by hand.

## laces

Lace is an embroidered fabric with cutout designs on a net background. It's also knitted, crocheted, or woven. Edges and flounces have scallops on one edge. Galloons are scalloped on both edges. Beading is a lace trim that has ribbons running through it. Motifs or medallions are cut from allover lace.

## novelty trims

Sequined and metallic braids, leather and vinyl strips, and embroidered and woven trims can be found in most notions departments. These can be removed from old clothes and stitched to new ones. Braid and ribbon bindings are used as a quick way to finish a raw edge.

## ribbing

Rib knit fabric is used to trim jacket collars, cuffs, and hems and is sold precut in packages. Ribbed trim can be cut from T-shirts, sweaters, or yard goods.

## ribbons

Grosgrain is a finely ribbed woven ribbon possessing a crispness and body, which lends itself well to belts and facings. Satin and taffeta ribbons are lighter and softer. Double-faced satin is perfect for bows and sashes. Stretch ribbons are best applied to stretch or knit garments. Stretch web is a wide elastic used for bands and belts. All these come in a variety of patterns, colors, and widths.

## threads

For general hand or machine stitching, cotton thread should be used on woven, natural fiber fabrics like cotton, linen, silk, and wool. Polyester should be used on synthetic fabrics, especially those with stretch. Cotton-wrapped polyester thread is less expensive and offers greater color choices than mercerized cotton, so its use for alteration projects is acceptable. Heavy-duty thread can be used for decorative topstitching. Embroidery floss is a loosely twisted six-strand thread used for hand embroidery.

## tulle

Tulle is a netlike fabric that varies in stiffness and weight. Attached to a slip, it creates volume under garments. It adds a decorative and glamorous element to hats, hems, and other items.

## yarn

Knitting yarn typically comes in wool or acrylic. Novelty yarns with other fiber content create interesting textures.

*Fusible web is a fun product used for turning an embroidered scarf into instant appliqués. (See Worn-out Flares to Pretty Pedal Pushers on page 45.)*

embroidered scarf

sewing thread

embriodery floss

fusible web

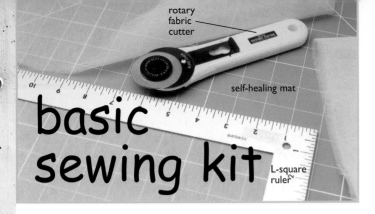

rotary fabric cutter

self-healing mat

# basic sewing kit

L-square ruler

**Proper tools** contribute to better results. You will need a surface on which to cut, pin, and sew. A folding cutting board (most sewing supply retailers sell these) protects a table from scratches and provides a working surface anywhere you choose to place it. A full-length mirror is invaluable when designing and fitting your own clothes.

## sewing machine

Any sewing machine in good working order can be used for alterations. Make sure that it's oiled and clean. A supply of different-sized needles and a zipper foot is a must. Use the needles with the smaller holes on finer, thin fabrics. The needles with large holes are best for heavier fabrics and trims. A machine that does a zigzag stitch is more versatile, and the zigzag stitch can be used to make buttonholes.

## beeswax

Used to strengthen thread for hand sewing and to reduce tangling and knotting.

## chalk

Chalk pencils and chalk wheels are used to mark fabrics and trims. They come in white and blue and can be brushed off, leaving no permanent marks. Other marking tools are useful, especially air-erasable ink.

## fine-tip marker

An indelible permanent marker such as a Flair or Sharpie is used to mark tape. (Don't use it on fabrics.)

## hand-sewing needles

Needles generally come packaged in assorted sizes. Sharps (#7 to #10) are used most often. Beading needles are long and fine, with small eyes. Yarn needles are thick, with blunt or sharp points and large eyes. Use a needle threader with a metal hook to pull yarn through the eye.

## iron and ironing board

An iron with temperature and steam controls works well on any fabric. Keep the soleplate clean at all times. A full-size or table-top ironing board is needed.

## measuring tape

A flexible measuring tool, the tape measure is used to obtain accurate measurements over curved areas.

## pins

Dressmaker #17 steel pins are good all-purpose pins. Silk pins are sharper and pierce fabric more easily.

## press cloth

A piece of finely woven sheer cotton or cheesecloth is used to protect the fabric from iron marks as well as protecting the iron when using fusible materials.

## rotary fabric cutter and self-healing mat

This tool cuts a perfectly smooth line, which is necessary when working with felt, tulle, and other items with raw-edge finishes.

## ruler

The 18" × 2" (45.7 × 5.1 cm) clear ruler and a yardstick are the most useful measuring tools for sewing. Special rulers are necessary when using a rotary cutter. An L-square is used when marking right angles. A small ruler is useful when turning up hems.

## scissors

Dedicate one pair of sharp scissors specifically for use with fabric. Using them for cutting other things such as paper will dull the blade. Dressmaker shears with a bent handle make it easier to slide along the table when cutting. Small embroidery scissors make trimming in delicate or hard-to-reach areas easier.

## seam ripper

Seam rippers cut the thread that joins seams. Parts of garments can be cleanly separated with their seam allowances intact. Use this sharp tool with care!

## twill tape

The ¼" (6 mm) cotton version of this tape has many uses. It's pinned onto garments to mark style lines. It's stitched into seams to stabilize and prevent stretching. Most knit garments have twill tape on the shoulder seams. It can also be used as a drawstring or for ties.

even running stitch

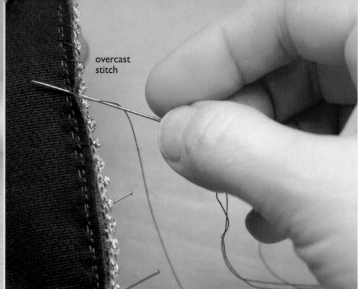

overcast stitch

# basic stitches

## hand stitches

### backstitch

This is a permanent hand stitch that's primarily used in places that are hard to reach with a sewing machine (A). It's often used to install zippers and to reinforce strained areas on a garment. It can be used as a decorative embroidery outline stitch. The complete stitch pattern consists of two parts: a full stitch forward and a half stitch back.

### blind hem stitch

This stitch is worked inside the hem for an invisible appearance. Tiny horizontal stitches alternate from below the hem edge, straight across to the garment (B).

### chainstitch

This is a flexible stitch that has some built-in stretch. It can be used to join seams or for embroidery. It can be made by hand or on a specialty machine. To make a hand chainstitch, start by pulling the thread to the surface. Make a loop, insert the needle back through the fabric in a spot right next to the entry point, and then let the needle tip emerge a short distance away. Keeping the thread loop under the needle, pull the needle through to the surface and snug the thread. When you make the next loop stitch, the first loop will be captured underneath (C).

### overcast stitch

When the seam is held vertically, this is a horizontal stitch. It's used to attach facings and hems. Sometimes it's referred to as a slant stitch because it forms a diagonal pattern along an edge. The overcast stitch can be used to keep fabric from fraying or as a decorative edging. The stitch shown at right is pictured finishing a hem that's edged with seam binding (D).

### running stitch

The even running stitch is used to hold seams together or layers in place (E). Tiny running stitches can be used as a permanent stitch while larger stitches, called basting, are used as temporary stitches.

The uneven running stitch is used to mark temporary style or placement lines on fabric (E). It can be used to indicate the right and wrong sides of fabric. This is done when a short stitch is taken on the right side and a long stitch is taken on the wrong side. When used as a permanent stitch for attaching appliqués, a tiny stitch is taken on the right side, with a longer stitch on the wrong side.

### slipstitch

This is an invisible stitch used to secure facings and hems and to match fabric patterns at seams. The needle slips through the fold of the top fabric, emerges, picks up a few threads of the garment and goes right back into the fold. The stitch shown at right is pictured finishing a wide bias bound hem (F).

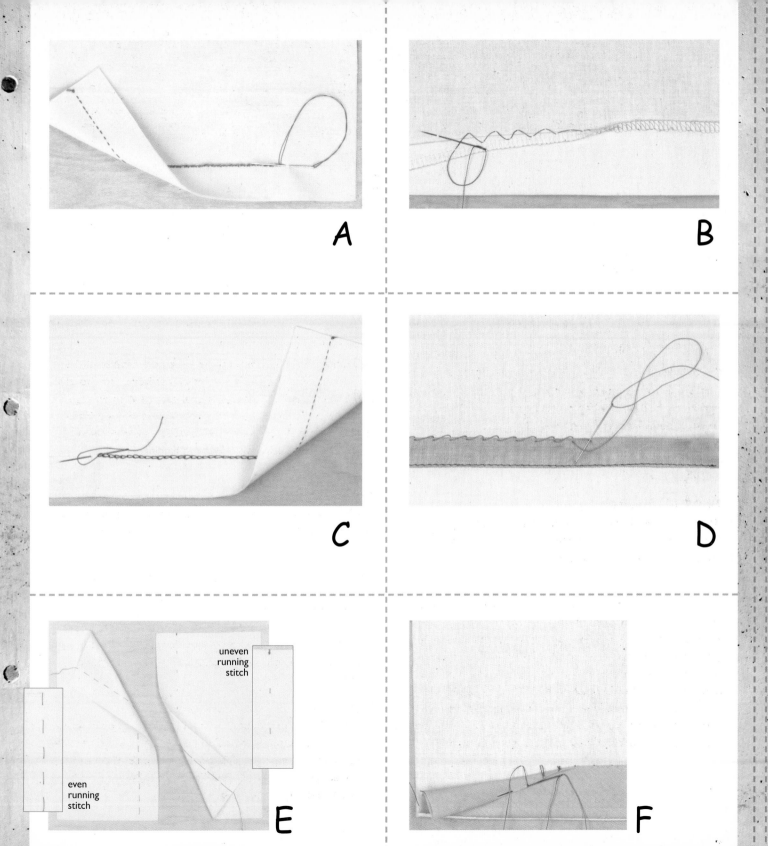

even
running
stitch

uneven
running
stitch

A

B

C

D

E

F

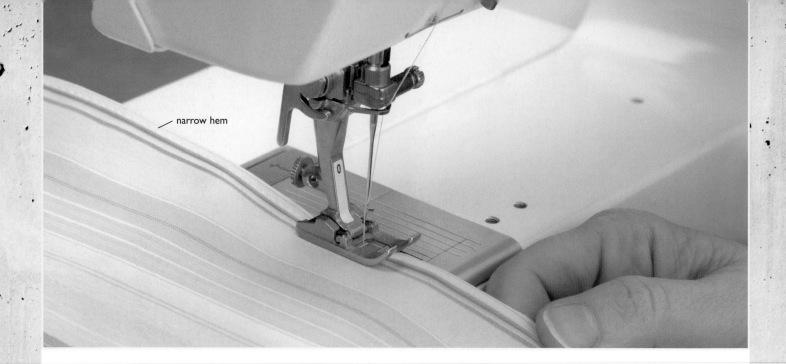

narrow hem

# machine stitches

### center zipper application

This is the most commonly used zipper application (G, 1). The seam is machine stitched below the place where the zipper will be positioned. The seam allowances are pressed back, along the zipper opening. With the zipper open, the coil or teeth are aligned just inside the seam allowance fold line. Each side of the zipper is pinned and basted in place. Using a zipper foot, the zipper is stitched down a side, with the stitching centered on the zipper tape. Near the bottom, the needle is left in the fabric, the zipper foot is raised, and the zipper tab (head) is pulled up past the needle to close the zipper. This is continued to the bottom, ending at the top of the seamline. Stitches are placed across, below the zipper staple. The thread is pulled through to the wrong side and knotted. The second side of the zipper is then sewn.

### edgestitch

This is a topstitching line that's positioned 1/16" (1.6 mm) or less from a finished edge (G, 4). It's used on collars, cuffs, plackets, hems, and belts.

### overlock stitch

A three-thread serger or overlock machine trims and finishes fabric edges on seam allowances, hems, and facings (G, 3).

### zigzag stitch

This stitch is used to finish fabric edges, such as seam allowances (G, 2). It's also used for attaching elastic and cord, as well as for a decorative stitch on garment parts and belts. To hold cord or elastic in place, the zigzag stitch straddles the filler, to encase it without stitching through it.

### gathering stitch

This stitch produces fullness in a given area. The first row of medium to long stitches should be close to the seamline of the garment. The second row is 1/4" (6 mm) away from the first, in the seam allowance. To gather the fabric, the bobbin threads are held at either end of the stitching and then the fabric is slid over the threads. The pulled bobbin thread ends are wrapped in a figure eight around pins at the end of the stitching, to hold the adjusted gathering in place (H).

### understitch

This stitch, which is made 1/8" (3 mm) from a seamline, joins seam allowances to a facing (I). Understitching pulls the facing seamline to the inside of the garment, rendering a clean, smooth edge on the right side. It's commonly used on neck, armhole, and waist facings.

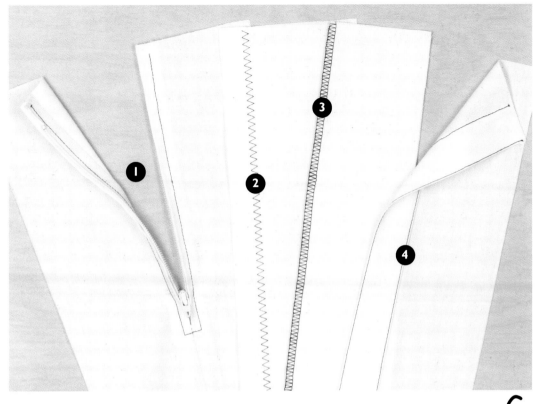

1. center zipper application
2. zigzag stitch
3. overlock stitch
4. edgestitch

*G*

*H*

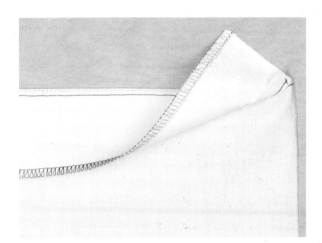

*I*

# interfacings and web

A woven, nonwoven, or knit backing is added to fabrics for stability and shaping (A). Interfacing can be sewn in or fused to a fabric with an iron. Fusible web is like a glue that joins fabric pieces together when dry heat is applied.

## fusible web

Similar in texture to interfacing, fusible web permanently adheres two fabric layers together with the heat of an iron (A, 1). This web is useful for working with appliqués, belts, and hems.

There are several types of fusible web on the market. Some products have a protective sheet on one side, so that you can fuse the web to one fabric, then peel off the sheet and apply it to the other fabric. Other types of fusible web are sandwiched between fabric layers and then fused at the same time.

## fusible weft interfacing

This interfacing has a dominant crosswise grain thread and adheres to only one side of the fabric (A, 2). It's strong, durable, and used to interface garments and facings. It adds medium-weight body to the fabric and it does fray.

## fusible tricot (knit) interfacing

Tricot is light and stretchy, which makes it a perfect interfacing for a knit garment. Tricot interfacing adheres to one side of the fabric, adds light body, and doesn't fray (A, 3).

## fusible woven interfacing

This is an all-purpose interfacing that's used on woven garments (A, 4). It comes in various weights and degrees of stiffness, adheres to one side of the fabric, and does fray.

# finishes

## single-fold bias tape

This fabric tape is used for finishing curved areas such as neck and armhole facings. It can also be used to make a narrow hem or a casing for tape or elastic (B). Single fold bias tape is used as a facing and as a casing in Flat '50s Frock to Flirty Fabulous Dress, on page 72.

## wide bias tape

Like single-fold bias tape (see the entry above), the long edges of wide bias tape are narrow folded to the inside. This tape is used for straight or slightly curved hems, and facings, and as a decorative binding or trim (B).

## narrow hem

A twice-folded hem, this treatment is typically ¼" (6 mm) wide for a shirt hem (C). The finished width can be ⅛" to ³/₁₆" (3 mm to 4.7 mm) wide for hems that are used on sashes, scarves, and ruffles.

## snap, hook, bar, and eye

Lightweight, wire hooks are used in delicate or narrow areas such as at the tops of zippers (D). Small snaps are used as closures in areas that are not highly strained such as the inside of a waistband, to hold extensions in place. Hooks and eyes, as well as snaps, can be used in place of zippers as long as the garment is loose fitting.

## skirt or trouser hook and bar

Sturdier than the wire hook, the skirt or trouser hook and bar are used as closures in highly strained areas such as waistbands and belts, for a firmer hold (D).

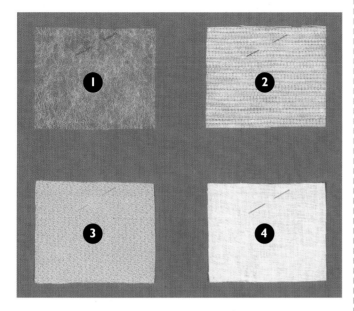

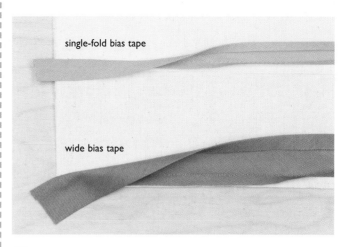

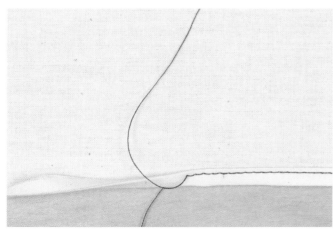

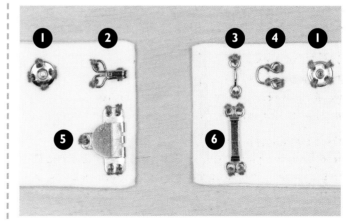

*A*

1. fusible web
2. fusible weft interfacing
3. fusible tricot knit interfacing
4. fusible woven interfacing

*B*

single-fold bias tape

wide bias tape

*C*

*D*

1. snap
2. hook
3. bar
4. eye
5. skirt or trouser hook
6. skirt or trouser bar

# TECHNIQUES

I often tell my students that there is more than one way to do anything when it comes to sewing. They surprise me sometimes with new ways of using classic techniques. Basic skills such as sewing on a button and stitching a hem will be covered in this section. Other topics include creatively reusing discarded garment parts.

## Bound Hem

Tailored linen vests and jackets are often unlined so that they're cool to wear in the summer. The seam allowances are usually bound with a lining-type fabric. When the hem on a garment like this is cut and shortened, you can use a bound hem to duplicate a couture look.

### materials

- basic sewing kit (see page 13)
- garment for hemming
- 1 yard (0.91 m) of rayon seam binding, color-matched to existing binding or garment
- sewing thread

### instructions

1. Preshrink the seam binding by rinsing it in a sink of warm water or by steam-pressing it (A). Allow the damp binding to dry thoroughly before using it.

2. Fold the binding lengthwise, not quite in half so that one side is 1/16" (1.6 mm) wider than the other (B).

3. Place the binding over the cut edge of the hem, with the wider side of the tape on the wrong side of the fabric. Hand baste it in place, through all of the fabric layers (C).

4. Again working through all of the fabric layers and with the right side of the garment face up, machine stitch, using a regular stitch length, close to the edge of the binding (D).

5. Fold up the hem allowance and finger-press a new hemline (E). Pin up the hem, with the pins parallel and close to the hemline. Use a blind hem stitch by rolling the bound edge back and taking a tiny right-to-left stitch on the inside of the binding and then moving to a new stitch position diagonally across, on the garment (F). Hem in a right-to-left direction.

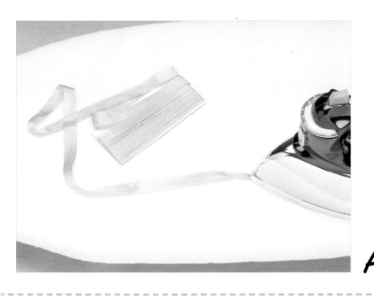

A

B

C

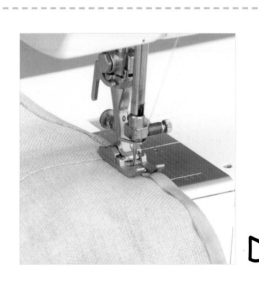

D

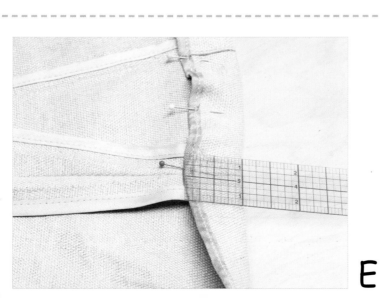

E

F

# Permanent Bow Belt

You can create a bow belt that never needs to be tied.

## materials

- basic sewing kit (see page 13)
- belt fabric or fabric belt from garment
- sewing thread, color-matched to the ribbon
- 2 hook-and-eye sets

## instructions

1. Cut the old belt or belt fabric to the waistline measurement plus 2" (5.1 cm) for ease and overlap. Finish the cut edges, mark, and sew on the hooks and eyes.

2. From the remaining belt, cut a 12½" (31.7 cm) piece, then tuck the ends inside and slipstitch them shut for the streamer. Cut a 14" (35.6 cm) piece, form a loop by overlapping the ends, and hand stitch the ends together.

3. Center the bow loop over the streamer piece, which is near the end of the belt where the hooks were stitched.

4. The remaining 5" (12.7 cm) will wrap around all layers at the center, acting as the knot. Adjust for a snug fit and hand stitch the overlapped ends.

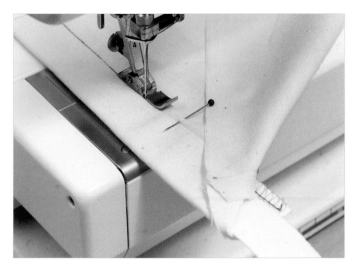

G

H

## Stitch-in-the-Ditch

This quick waistband finish saves time, reduces thickness at the waist, and produces a neat finish inside.

### materials

- basic sewing kit (see page 13)
- garment
- waistband cut out of fabric
- I yard (0.9 m) of I" (25 mm) -wide elastic
- sewing thread, color-matched to the fabric

### instructions

1. Trim and finish one seam allowance of the waistband to measure ¼" (6 mm) wide with an overlock or zigzag stitch, or bind the edge.

2. Pin and stitch the unfinished edge of the waistband to the garment, with the right sides together. Turn and press the seam allowance up toward the waistband. Fold the waistband over, to the inside, for the finished width. (Waistbands should be interfaced if they are not housing elastic.) Pin the finished edge in place, dropped ¼" (6 mm) below the waist seam. The finished edge is not turned under.

3. With a zipper foot, machine straight stitch along the waist seamline. Adjust the needle and foot to get close enough to stitch in the seam (ditch) ( G). (The photo for this step is a cross section showing the waist seam, its seam allowance, the inserted elastic, and the machine stitching technique. The steps give instructions for using this technique on a skirt or pants [H].) Leave a 1½" (3.8 cm) opening through which to pull and attach the elastic ends. Cut the elastic to the desired length, enter through the opening, and pull through with a safety pin on one end. Overlap and stitch the elastic ends. Stitch in the seam to close the waistband completely.

# Rosebud

An elastic waist that has been cut off of a gathered skirt can become a flower. This feminine accessory can be pinned to a dress or belt or stitched to a bag or headpiece.

## materials

- basic sewing kit (see page 13)
- elastic waistband, cut off a garment
- ¼ yard (0.2 m) of ⅞" (22 mm) -wide ribbon for base and leaves
- sewing thread, color-matched to the ribbon
- small pin back to attach rosebud to garment
- hot glue gun (optional)
- leaf base pattern (see page 126)

  Note: The elastic in the waistband needs to be ½" (13 mm) wide or narrower, otherwise your rose will look like a cabbage.

## instructions

1.  If you haven't already cut the waistband off the skirt, do so now (I). Make sure that there's 1¼" (3.2 cm) of fabric extending below the bottom of the elastic. If the elastic is loose inside the waistband casing, make a line of straight stitching through the width of the waistband casing on both sides of both side seams. Cut through the waist elastic at one of the side seams (J) to open the circle.

2.  Trim the ruffle to ½" (1.3 cm) at one end and gradually increase the width to 1" (2.5 cm) at the other end.

3.  Do not hem the raw edge, which will become the petal edges. Start by firmly rolling the narrow end (K). Continue rolling, to finish with the wide end, to form a bud.

4.  Hand stitch the rolled end (elastic edge) together, overlapping the stitches to secure all of the layers (L).

5.  Trim the outer petal end into a curve. Cut and fold the ribbon ends under to form the bud base and leaves. Pin and hand stitch the ribbon in place. A pin back may be stitched or glued to the bottom.

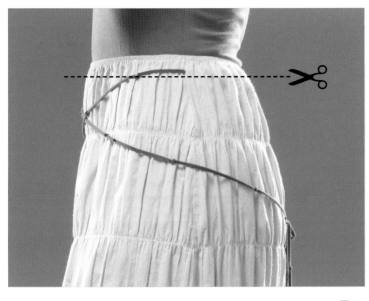

I

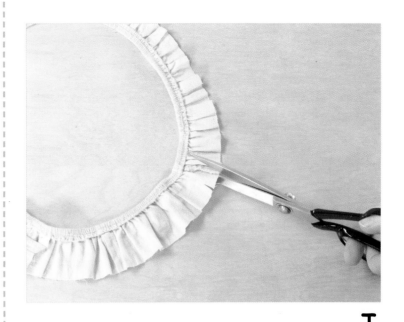

J

K

L

## Thread Belt Carrier

New belts are created for many of the garments in this book. Existing belt carriers may be broken and need to be replaced or relocated. A thread chain in a matching color offers a neat, nearly invisible solution.

### materials

- basic sewing kit (see page 13)
- garment
- belt
- sewing or buttonhole twist thread, color-matched to the garment

### instructions

1. Try on the garment together with the belt. Mark the belt's position by placing a pin above and below the belt. Generally, belt carriers are placed at the side seams but they can be placed wherever additional support is needed. Allow ⅛" (3 mm) ease both above and below the belt width.

2. Using a double thread on a hand sewing needle, fasten the thread securely on the inside seam allowance at the first pin (M).

3. Bring the needle out through the seam to the right side. Take a short stitch at the seamline to form a thread loop (N).

4. Hold the needle with your right hand. Slip the thumb and index finger of the opposite hand through the loop and pick up the needle thread. Pull the thread through the first loop to form a new loop (O). Don't pull through the needle (P).

5. Continue in this manner, keeping the chain loops an even size until the chain is the desired length (Q). Try wrapping the length around the belt to ensure a perfect fit.

6. Place the needle through the loop and pull the thread to form a knot (R).

7. Bring the needle through the seam, back to the wrong side at the other pin marker (S). Secure the thread with several tiny backstitches on the seam allowance (T).

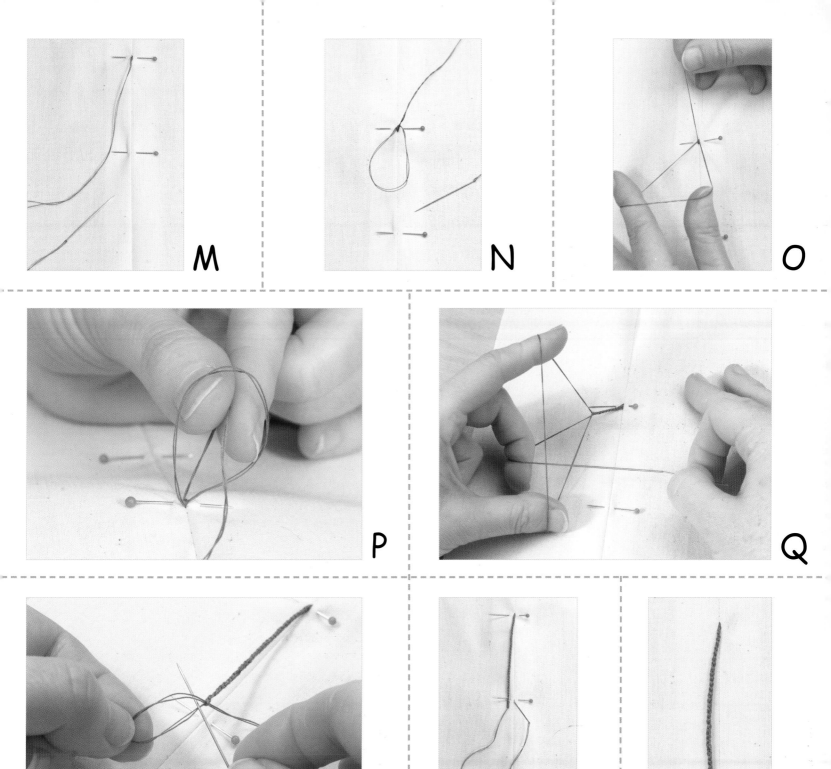

M

N

O

P

Q

R

S

T

# Thread Shank

Do your coat buttons fall off soon after you've stitched them back on? One reason may be that the button needs to be stitched on with an allowance for thick fabric. These instructions are written specifically for two- or four-hole buttons that do not have shanks on their undersides.

## materials

- basic sewing kit (see page 13)
- garment
- button
- sewing or buttonhole twist thread, color-matched to the garment
- toothpick
- paper toweling

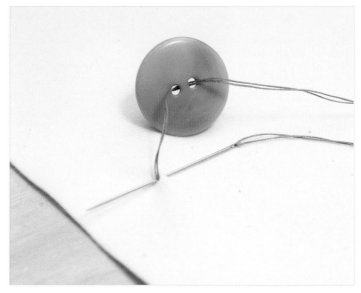

U

## instructions

1. Cut a length of thread and run it through beeswax. Press the thread between paper toweling to force the beeswax into the thread fibers. This will reduce tangling while sewing and strengthen the thread. Thread a needle and knot the two ends of the thread together. If possible, slip the needle between the facing and the top of the garment so that the knot is inside. Otherwise, take a tiny stitch at the point where the button will be placed, through all layers. The knot is on the right side of the garment, at the base of the button. (Two small backstitches can also be used instead of a knot.)

2. Bring the needle up at the exact point where the button is to be placed, go through one hole in the button, across the top, and back down through the opposite hole. Take the next stitch, through all fabric layers, bringing the needle back up to the right side of the garment (U). Don't pull the thread tight.

3. Once the button is anchored in step 2, create a thread shank by placing a toothpick under the first stitch across the top of the button. Take three or four more stitches over the toothpick and through the holes and fabric (V).

4. Remove the toothpick (W).

5. Slide the button up (X).

6. Circle the button, wrapping the thread around the vertical threads four times. On the last turn, form a loop. Slide the needle through the loop and pull it to form a knot at the base of the button. Take a tiny stitch and then lose the thread end by sliding the needle between the fabric layers and cutting the threads close to where they surface (Y).

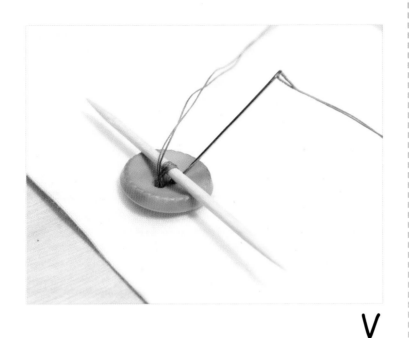

V

W

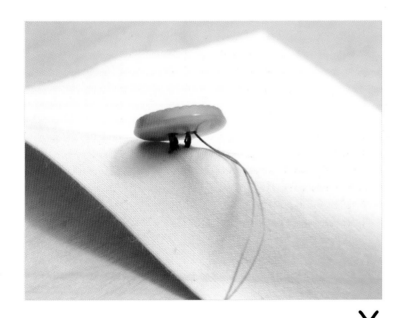

X

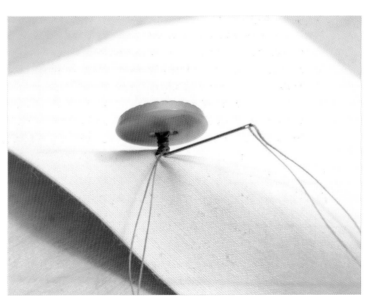

Y

# projects

**To Begin**, flip through the following pages to view a collection of worn clothes that have been altered. Before and after images, along with step-by-step instructions, make it easier to achieve each makeover. Projects have been rated for **sewing skill level,** starting with one star for beginner, two stars for intermediate, and three for advanced. All materials used can be found in the resource list in the back of the book.

AFTER

# STAINED SKIRT TO WAVY WONDER

White clothes that are hopelessly stained are perfect candidates for experimentation. Who knows? They may be able to be worn again. Natural fibers such as pure linen, cotton, or silk dyes easily. Before dyeing this linen circle skirt red, rows of cord were stitched around the skirt to emphasize flow and movement inherent in this swinging style.

**BEFORE**

**LEVEL OF SKILL:** ⭐

### materials

- basic sewing kit (see page 13)
- circle skirt
- 10 yards (9.1 m) of #24 soft white twisted or cable cord
- white cotton sewing thread
- ½ yard (0.5 m) of white linen for a test swatch
- satin, zigzag, or special-purpose presser foot that has a groove on the bottom
- clear or frosted tape (optional, see step 8)
- fabric dye in 2 similar colors, 1 package of powder or ½ bottle of liquid in each color (you may need more dye if your skirt is more than 3 yards (2.7 m) of fabric or you want medium, bright, or dark results)
- 2 cups (500 ml) of table or sea salt
- 2 tablespoons (28 ml) of laundry detergent
- rubber gloves
- stainless steel bucket, tub, or kitchen sink for dyeing
- chlorine bleach to rinse bucket, tub, or sink immediately after dyeing
- safety glasses
- plastic drop cloth

Note: Skirt shown in photo was dyed with Rit dye colors Scarlet and Wine.

## instructions

1. Make a test sample by cutting an 18" X 28" (45.7 X 71.1 cm) swatch which is the same fiber content as the skirt. Select the zigzag stitch on the sewing machine. Set the stitch length to 2.5 (12 spi, or stitches per inch) and the width to 5 (very wide). Make sure to use a satin, zigzag, or other special-purpose presser foot that has a groove along the entire length of the bottom for this project. Don't choose a presser foot that requires you to feed the cord through a coil or tunnel on the front of the toe. Zigzag around the edges of the swatch to stabilize fraying.

2. Wash and dry the garment, swatch, and cord in order to preshrink the materials and remove any finish that would prevent the fibers from absorbing the dye. You may want to experiment with other types of cords or trims on the sample. Pin the cord in a snakelike pattern on the swatch (A).

3. With the swatch already on the sewing machine bed, center the cord under the presser foot with a few inches extending out the back of the foot. (Hold this end for the first few stitches, to ensure a smooth start-up.) Loosen the top thread tension by one setting (refer to your machine manual for adjustments). The zigzag stitch needs to be wide enough to clear both sides of the cord, and loose enough that the stitches don't pucker or pull down the top of the cord (B). As you stitch, you are creating a thread tunnel under which the cord will run. Practice stitching over the cords, removing the pins

   as you sew. Hold the fabric taut, almost stretching it, as you sew, to prevent puckering. If you find there's a lot of puckering, loosen the needle tension another setting.

4. To dye the sample swatch, use a small amount of the dye and carefully follow the manufacturer's instructions. It's a good idea to wear rubber gloves and safety glasses during the process, to shield you from any skin irritation. Dye the fabrics in a stainless steel bucket, tub, or kitchen sink. You will need plenty of water to rinse after the dyeing process. When the sample is dry, check the results. If you're pleased with how it looks, you are ready to work on the real thing.

5. If a sash belt is attached to the skirt, secure it out of the way during the process of pinning and sewing the cord. Remember to release the sash before dyeing, so that it absorbs the color evenly.

6. Measure 2½" (6.4 cm) up the left side seam from the skirt hem, open the seam ½" (1.3 cm), and insert one end of the cord into the seam (C). Secure the cord end to the inside seam allowance by machine stitching the seam closed over the cord. Spread the front skirt flat on the table.

7. Lay the cord on the skirt in a freeform wave pattern near the bottom of the skirt (D).

8. Pin the cord in place every few inches or centimeters (D). You can also use small pieces of clear or frosted tape.

## Tip

Don't worry if you can't find the exact cord called for in the instructions. A #24 cord is ³⁄₁₆" (4.7 mm) thick. Just look for a cotton cord that's thick enough to be visible when it's stitched to the skirt. Make sure that it isn't too thick— the cord needs to fit in the groove on the underside of the presser foot.

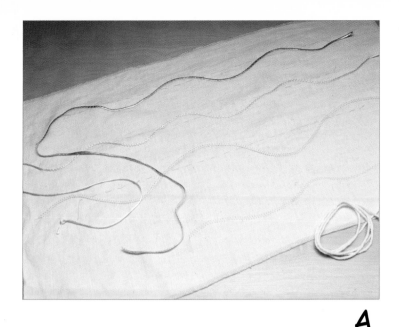

A

B

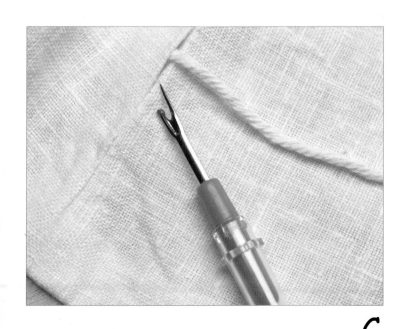

C

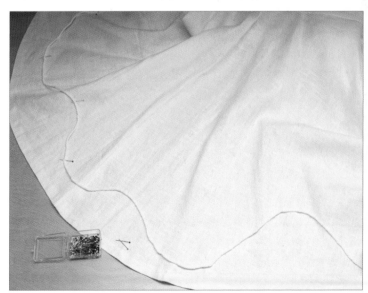

D

**9.** Gently turn the skirt around to the back. Continue to pin the cord as on the front and let your design spiral around the front and back until there are three rows of cord "snaked" around the skirt (E). Insert the end of the cord into the seam the same way it started near the hem.

**10.** You do not want to run out of thread in the middle of the appliqué process (attaching the cord to the skirt), so begin sewing with a full bobbin. It should be the same cotton thread as the spool on top. Machine zigzag the cord to the skirt. Do not stitch over the pins. Remove them just before the needle reaches them. You can stitch over tape, but make sure it doesn't leave a sticky residue on the needle. (This can be removed with adhesive remover, but make sure to then wipe the needle with vinegar so that the cleaner doesn't stain your skirt.) When the stitching is complete, end your sewing without backstitching, break the threads leaving long tails, pull the top threads through to the inside, and tie them off in a knot.

**11.** Prepare the dye bath for the skirt with a full box (or half a bottle) of the lighter color dye. The dye may stain your tub or floor, although washing it immediately with chlorine bleach will reduce the staining. You may want to cover the floor or worktable with a plastic drop cloth. Place the skirt in the dye bath and color it by carefully following the manufacturer's instructions (F).

**12.** Do this step while the skirt is still wet. To achieve an ombré effect with a deeper, more intense color at the hem, dye the bottom of the skirt a darker shade. The wine dye color was used in the example in the photos. Repeat the process but hold the waistline out of the dye (G) and gradually lift until the hem is visibly darker (H).

**13.** Hang the skirt to drip dry in a shower or bathtub. (Drips from the dye may stain, so protect bathroom surfaces with a plastic drop cloth.) When the skirt is almost dry, press it from the wrong side with the cord face down on a towel, on the ironing board.

# Tips

• To accentuate the cord, use thread a shade darker than the color of the skirt hem and straight stitch along the side of the cord using a zipper foot.

• Although linen is ideal because it accepts dye readily, a skirt in any all-natural fabric is suitable for dyeing. If the skirt is colored already, you can strip the color with Rit Color Remover, and then proceed with the new color.

• Some all-natural garments are sewn together with polyester thread, which won't accept dye as readily as the fabric.

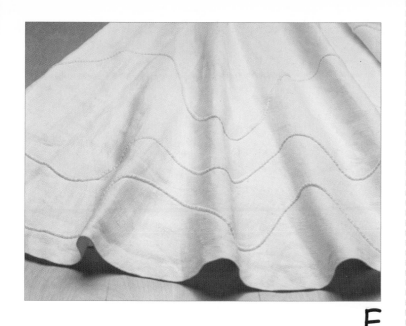

E

F

G

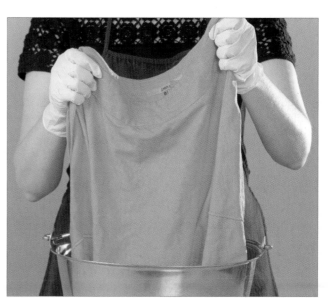

H

# QUIET TUNIC TO SPIRITED VEST

Beautifully tailored inside and out, this thrift store find
needed new life breathed into it. A newer proportion
with a splash of color and polish makes this vest shine.

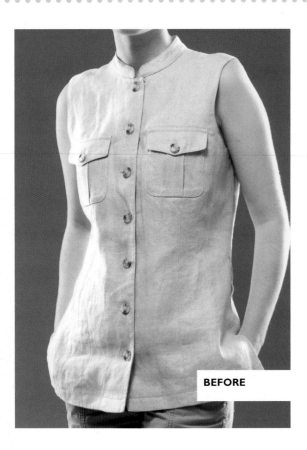

**BEFORE**

## LEVEL OF SKILL: ★★

### materials

- basic sewing kit (see page 13)
- sleeveless tunic with mandarin collar
- 1 yard (0.9 m) of rayon seam binding, color-matched to the tunic
- 1½ yards (1.4 m) of 1⅜" (35 mm) -wide grosgrain ribbon for the belt and epaulettes
- 1 yard (0.9 m) of 1⅜" (35 mm) -wide grosgrain ribbon in contrasting color for the belt underside
- 2 yards (1.8 m) of ¾" (1.9 cm) -wide fusible web
- sewing thread, color-matched to the fabric
- sewing thread, color-matched to the grosgrain ribbon
- 11 military-theme buttons, the same diameter as the ones on the tunic
- 1⅜" (3.5 cm) -wide metal buckle and tip set
- pliers
- several sheets of white tissue paper

AFTER

## instructions

1. To shorten the tunic, measure from the hem up to the lowest buttonhole (A), which is a length of 4" (10.2 cm) on this tunic. Remove the button that corresponds to this lowest button-hole and mark a chalk line parallel to the hem all the way around the garment (B). Try on the tunic to make sure that you like the new length. Cut off the hem along the chalk line (C). When your vest is finished, the new hemline will be about 1" (2.5 cm) above the cutting line.

2. Try the garment on in front of a mirror to check the fit. Place a pin at the waist. Pin along the side seam if it needs to be taken in. Make sure the right and left sides are taken in the same amount. Take the tunic off, turn it inside out, and chalk-mark along the pin lines, front and back. Remove the pins and press the seam allowances closed so they lay flat. Remove the belt carriers at the waist and release the armhole facing if it is tacked down at the side seam (D).

3. To mark a seamline for a new side seam, measure ½" (1.3 cm) in from the side seam at the waist and mark with a chalk wheel. Using a ruler, extend the chalk line up and taper it to nothing at the armhole seamline. From the waist to the hem, mark a line parallel to the curve of the pin-marked section, then chalked, side seam. Machine straight stitch the side seam.

4. Using a seam ripper, open up both side seams. Press the seam allowances open. Reattach the armhole facing to the side seam allowance with a few hand stitches. Following the Bound Hem instructions on page 20, attach the seam binding to the new hem edge that you cut in a previous step.

5. Pin the bottom 1" (2.5 cm) of the garment to the inside to establish the new hemline (E). Button the front of the gar-ment closed to make sure the right and left hems are even at the bottom. Stitch the hem.

6. Press the ribbons with lots of steam and let them dry in order to preshrink them. To make the epaulettes (shoulder tabs), cut two pieces of ribbon, each one the length of the shoulder seam plus 2" (5.1 cm).

7. Fold the ribbon in half lengthwise. At only one end of each ribbon, stitch across with a ¼" (6 mm) seam allowance (F).

A

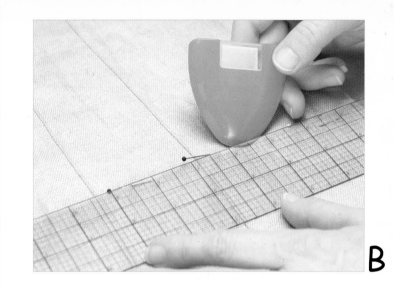

B

C

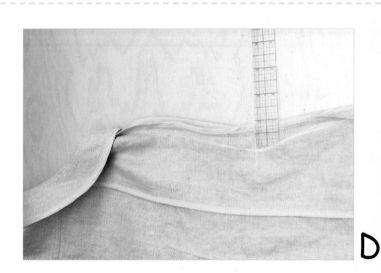

D

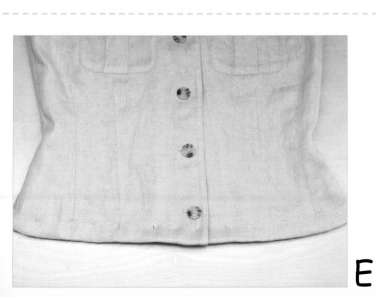

E

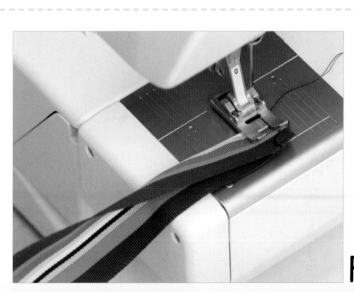

F

8. Diagonally trim the seam allowance at the point (the folded side). Press the seam allowance open. Turn the point right side out and press the ribbon so that the point is centered at one end and the seamline isn't visible (G). Prepare the second epaulette, with the remaining ribbon, in the same manner.

9. Center the length of the right side of an epaulette over the wrong side of a shoulder seam. Align the raw edge of the ribbon with the armhole edge. Hand stitch across the ribbon through all layers (including the armhole facing if the garment has one), ½" (1.3 cm) in from the raw edge of the ribbon (H).

10. Bring the epaulette out to the right side, with the point to the neckline seam. Mark a dot 1" (2.5 cm) in from the point using a chalk marking pencil. Tack the epaulette to the shoulder by making two or three tiny stitches near the neck, through all layers. Stitch the button on at that spot. Hand stitch each side of the ribbon to the facing on the inside of the armhole to hold the epaulette firmly in place.

11. Along the front opening, carefully remove all the buttons with a sharp seam ripper. Leave a thread or two to mark each spot for the new buttons. When replacing the buttons, make sure the new buttons fit through the buttonholes. Even though the diameter might be the same, a thicker button needs a longer buttonhole. Always buy an extra, in case you lose one. (Sew it to the inside of the side seam, near the hem. This way, it's always on hand if needed.)

12. Put on the vest and measure your waist—over the vest—with a measuring tape to determine the belt length.

Add 2" (5.1 cm) for the buckle end and 3" to 6" (7.6 to 15.2 cm) for the extension on the other end. Cut two lengths of the ribbon (one from the plain ribbon for the belt underside) and the fusible web, the length of the belt.

13. Lay a piece of tissue paper on the ironing board to protect it during the fusing process. Sandwich the fusible web between the wrong side of the ribbons as follows: Lay the first strip of web on top of the contrasting ribbon, flush with the ribbon edge. Repeat the process on the other edge. The web may overlap slightly in the center. Starting on one end, carefully lay the belt ribbon on top. Make sure all ribbon edges align perfectly. If necessary, hold the layers in place by pushing pins through the ribbon and the ironing board pad. Use pins with glass, not plastic, heads. Lightly press all of the layers together to hold the ribbons in place (I). Then, remove any pins and press from the center out to the sides. Hold the iron in place for a few seconds at a time for a firm fuse. Do not slide the iron along the surface. Use a press cloth to protect the ribbon.

14. Machine stitch through all the layers, close to each long edge of the belt. Stitch and trim the belt ends as well. Fold one end under ¾" (1.9 cm) and again 1" (2.5 cm), and clamp the buckle onto it (J). Use pliers to clamp the metal tip in place on the other end. This end can also be turned twice and hemmed with a machine stitch if there is no metal tip.

15. Belt carriers can be created by making a chain thread loop (K). (See page 28.)

G

H

I

J

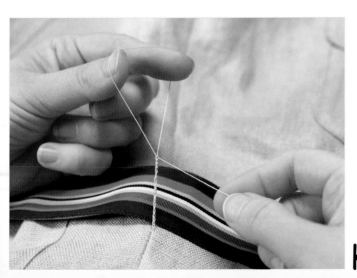

K

AFTER

# WORN-OUT FLARES TO PRETTY PEDAL PUSHERS

Favorite jeans generally show signs of wear on the knees and seat. No longer wearable because of the torn back, Holly donated hers for a makeover. The jeans are cut just below the knee where the cargo pockets are stitched. The pockets become a reversible tote bag and the jeans morph into chic short pants. An appliquéd belt always stays in place.

**BEFORE**

**LEVEL OF SKILL:** ★

**materials**

- basic sewing kit (see page 13)
- cargo jeans
- embroidered scarf
- ½ yard (0.5 m) of fusible web
- ½ yard (0.5 m) of fusible weft interfacing
- sewing thread, color-matched to the jeans
- sewing thread, color-matched to the embroidered scarf
- skein of embroidery floss to match or contrast with the embroidered scarf
- zigzag presser foot
- hand sewing embroidery needle
- 8" (20.3 cm) square of corrugated cardboard

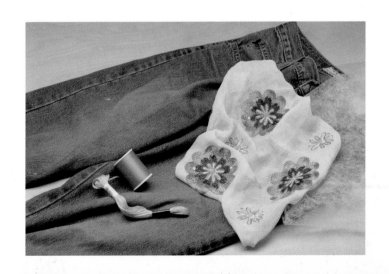

A

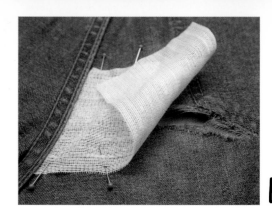

B

## instructions

1. Fold the pants on the center front crease lines. Mark the cutting line across the legs at the desired length with chalk, and cut off the lower pant legs. In the photo shown, the legs are cut along the top of the cargo pocket flap (A). Reserve the lower legs for patches and the tote bag (see pages 46–48). On the lower legs, measure and mark 1" (2.5 cm) up from the pant leg hems and cut off the bottom for use later as tote bag handles.

2. To patch the back seat, cut a piece of fabric from the bottom of the pant leg. Make the patch large enough to cover the tear all the way around. To patch both sides, cut two pieces from the cutoff leg, each 3½" × 6" (8.9 × 15.2 cm). Match the grain of the fabric to the grain of the pants. If necessary, trim the patch to fit beside (not over) the seamline and pocket.

3. Use the patch as a pattern to cut a piece of interfacing that will cover the tear on the wrong side. Trim the interfacing ¼" (6 mm) smaller than the outside (jean fabric) patch. Turn the pants inside out and place them on an ironing board. Center the interfacing over the tear and press in place, using a press cloth and no steam (B).

4. Turn the pants right side out. Machine zigzag stitch with a 4 width (wide) and 1 length (18 spi) several rows over the tear until it is closed up and all the loose threads are held down (C). Note: The contrasting thread used for zigzag stitching in the photo is for enhanced visibility only. Straight stitch around the edges of the interfacing to secure it in place.

5. Back the denim patch with fusible web. The embroidered appliqués can be cut from the embroidered scarf and backed with fusible web at the same time. Leave about ½" (1.3 cm) of scarf fabric around all edges of the appliqués (D).

6. Place the denim patch on the right side of the pants, over the stitch lines made for the inside patch. Don't bother turning under the edges of the patch. Fuse the patch in place (E). Using thread that's matched to the color of the pants, zigzag around the patch edges with a ½ length (20 spi) and 5 width (very wide) stitch, and pull all thread ends through to the wrong side and tie them off.

7. Embroider the patches around the edges using a buttonhole stitch and three strands of embroidery floss (F) and (G). Make and attach more jeans patches as desired. Ordinarily, the buttonhole stitch is made so that the thick line of connected stitches is along the edge. For this project, it is reversed (H).

8. Trim off the excess fabric around the outer edges of each appliqué. Pin the appliqués on the pants, below the pocket opening. Place a piece of cardboard between the pocket and the outside to keep from pinning through the pockets. Hand baste the pieces in place with a few large stitches. Test a scrap before pressing to make sure the heat does not melt or warp the sequins or decorative threads on the appliqués. Fuse the appliqués in place using a press cloth (I). You can also fuse them from the wrong side, with the pants facedown on a towel.

9. Hand stitch the appliqués in place using small running stitches and sewing thread (J). Make a chainstitch (see page 14), using embroidery floss, to link the appliqués.

10. Machine straight stitch around each leg, ½" (1.3 cm) up from the cut edge for the pant hem. Use a pin to pull down the crosswise grain threads to create a fringed edge below the stitching. When the thread is pulled as far as it can go, cut it at the stitch line.

C

D

E

F

G

H

I

J

# Pocketed Tote

AFTER

**LEVEL OF SKILL:** ★★

## materials

- basic sewing kit (see page 13)
- flare pant legs with cargo pockets
- heavy, thick sweater
- 1½ yards (1.4 m) of 1" (25 mm) -wide grosgrain ribbon matched to the sweater
- 1 yard (0.91 m) of 2" (5.1 cm) -wide belting, buckram, or stiff (craft) interfacing
- sewing thread, color-matched to the jeans
- sewing thread, color-matched to the sweater
- 1⅜" (3.5 cm) button
- bag body pattern (see page 127)
- button loop pattern (see page 128)
- handle pattern (see page 128)

*A*

B

C

## instructions

1. Measure 12" (30.5 cm) from the top of the pocket flap down the side seam, mark, and cut off the bottom of the pant leg. Make each leg into a flat piece of fabric by cutting it open vertically along the seam that's closest to the left side of one pocket edge and the right side of the other pocket edge. If you didn't cut off the hem when you made the pedal pushers (see page 46), do so now. Measure and mark 1" (2.5 cm) up from the hems and cut off the bottom for use as the tote bag handle. Repeat this step on the other leg. Refer to the pattern on page 127 as you complete the rest of this step. Place the legs so the pockets lay side by side. Space them ½" (1.3 cm) apart at the top of the pocket and 1¼" (3.2 cm) apart at the bottom of the pocket. Where the fabric overlaps, fold back both edges so that the folds butt together. Pin and mark a center front seam along the folds. Measure 14" (35.6 cm) across the top (this will be the front of the bag), pin, and mark a center back seam. The bag is slightly wider at the bottom to follow the shape of the flare leg. Machine stitch the center front and center back seams. Machine stitch the front to the back, wrong sides together, to make the bottom seam.

2. Turn the sweater upside down, placing the ribbed hem edge at the top of the bag. Cut the sweater, using the denim bag as the pattern, to the same length and width but placing the sweater seams on the bag's sides rather than center front and center back. Sew the side and bottom seams of the sweater.

3. Working on the sweater and jeans separately, form a base. At each corner, fold across the bottom, perpendicular to the seam, forming a triangle on the wrong side. Measure down from each point 2½" (6.4 cm), chalk-mark a line, and machine

stitch across it through all layers (A). Trim the seam allowances to ½" (13 mm).

4. Interface the mouth of the bag by pinning belting, buckram, or a strip of stiff interfacing ¼" (6 mm) below the cut edge. Overlap the ends.

5. Cut two pieces of grosgrain ribbon, each 22" (55.9 cm) long, for the bag handles (the grosgrain and pant hem pieces should be the same length). Machine stitch the cut, 1" (2.5 cm) wide, pant hem to the ribbon. Attach and pin the ends midway between the centers and sides at the top of the bag. Place the ribbon side so that it will match the knit inside (A).

6. For the button loop closure, cut a strip 1¼" × 6½" (3.2 × 16.5 cm) on the lengthwise grain of the leftover pant fabric. Fold ¼" (6 mm) to the wrong side along both long edges. Fold the strip in half along the length, so that the long folded edges match. Sew together close to the folded edges. Fold the finished strip in half across the width to form a loop. Place each end of the loop side by side with the seamlines facing each other. Machine stitch across the bottom of both ends and again ½" (1.3 cm) down from the top. Pin the loop at the top of the bag at center back. Machine stitch around the bag's mouth to secure the interfacing, handles, and button loop in place.

7. Place the knit bag inside the pant bag. Pin the edges and hand stitch them together with an overcast stitch. It's okay if the pant fabric is slightly frayed along the top edge and handles (B).

8. Stitch the button to the top front edge, between the pockets. A flat button requires a ¼" (6 mm) -long thread shank (see page 28) so the bag can be buttoned from either side (C).

AFTER

# Passé Poncho to Swinging Skirt

Last season's maternity poncho, knit in a simple purl stitch pattern, had a warm cuddly feel but did not look new anymore. It serves as a blank canvas for any type of yarn embroidery. Any full-length poncho can be used to make a skirt like this, as long as the neckline will stretch enough to slide down your body to the waist.

**BEFORE**

**LEVEL OF SKILL:** ⭐

### materials

- basic sewing kit (see page 13)
- poncho, no less than 23" (58.4 cm) long from the side of the neck (at the shoulder) to the hem at center front
- 1 skein of metallic gold-flecked yarn
- 1 skein of metallic silver-flecked yarn
- sewing thread, color-matched to the poncho
- 12 large gold paillettes
- tapestry needle
- needle threader
- masking tape (Safe-Release) or Handy Tape, Stick-a-ruler, or Tiger Tape
- wide-tooth comb

Note: Make sure that the paillettes and yarns can be washed and dried the same way that you care for the poncho.

## instructions

1. Place a poncho on the table and straighten the front fringed edge. Comb through the fringe and then place tape along the fringe ends on both sides to hold them in place during the embroidery process. Trim the fringe along the tape edge if it's uneven. To create an even hand stitch along the knit edge, make a guideline by laying a 1" (2.5 cm) -wide yardstick or ruler along the knitted edge of the poncho. Set the masking tape on the right side of the fabric, along the ruler edge. Using the felt-tip pen, mark the tape at ¾" (1.9 cm) increments. Later, this process will need to be repeated for the sides and back of the poncho, reusing the marked tape at each location.

2. Use a needle threader to pull the ends of the silver and gold yarns together through the eye of the tapestry needle (A and B).

3. Knot the yarn ends and start with the knot on the wrong side of the knit edge, at the far right end of the masking tape. If you're worried that a knot will pull through the knitted fabric, tie the end around an existing yarn strand in the poncho.

   To create the diagonal stitch, start by bringing the needle and thread out to the right side of the fabric just below the lower edge of the masking tape, at the first pen mark. Take a diagonal stitch by inserting the needle through the fabric near the edge of the poncho, below—and directly in line with—the second mark on the masking tape. Take a stitch under the fabric, from the knit edge to the second mark on the masking tape (C). Do not pull the yarn tight or the edge will curl. Working on a tabletop will help keep work flat as you go. Continue to work around the hem edge until it is complete. Tie it off and neaten the yarn ends when finished. Weave in the yarn ends on the wrong side when the stitching is complete.

4. Plan where you would like to place the embroidery stitches and paillettes on the poncho surface. To make a Lazy Daisy stitch, start with a knot on the inside of the poncho. Bring the needle out, form a loop and insert it back into the same hole. Slide the needle underneath 1" to 2" (2.5 to 5.1 cm) and let the needle tip poke out the right side of the fabric surface (D).

5. Make sure that the needle tip is inside the loop made in the last step. Pull the needle and thread through to the right side of the fabric and make a small stitch over the loop end (E). Bring the needle up at the original, center point and repeat the process to form three more petals.

6. Bring the needle up in the center and slide a large paillette onto the yarn (F). Secure the paillette with a backstitch.

7. Finish the yarn ends on the outside to create a stem effect (G).

8. For the drawstring waist, cut double the amount of yarn needed for a dropped waistline plus a tie. Have a partner hold one end while the other twists the yarns to tighten the twist. Hold the center of the length and walk slowly toward your partner. Lower the center as you move together. The yarn will twist on itself to create a double-twist cord. Thread the cord through a needle and then weave the needle and thread in and out of the poncho, around the neck edge, starting and ending at center front. Knot the tie at the ends (H). The neck will stretch enough to slide down to the waist. Tie the drawstring and adjust it to fit properly.

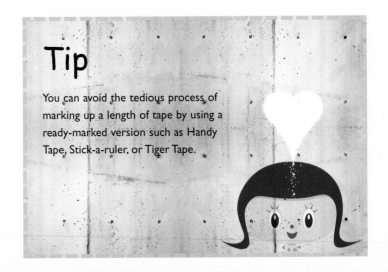

## Tip

You can avoid the tedious process of marking up a length of tape by using a ready-marked version such as Handy Tape, Stick-a-ruler, or Tiger Tape.

A

B

C

D

E

F

G

H

# PRECIOUS PULLOVER TO CLASSY CARDIGAN

Although this pullover is a fine acrylic knit, it has the look and feel of cashmere. The neck has stretched out and the ribbed hem is too tight. By cutting it into a cardigan, its life has been extended and made into a more versatile wardrobe piece, perfect for work, or over jeans on a night out.

**BEFORE**

**LEVEL OF SKILL:** ★★

## materials
- basic sewing kit (see page 13)
- finely knit cardigan
- 3 yards (2.7 m) of ⅞" (22 mm) -wide stretch velvet ribbon
- cotton-wrapped polyester sewing thread, color-matched to the sweater
- sewing thread, color-matched to the ribbon
- 6 buttons
- 2 large hook-and-eye sets
- 2 cardboard strips (optional): one that's as long as the sweater and several inches wide, and another that's slightly narrower than the sweater sleeve and 8" (20.3 cm) long

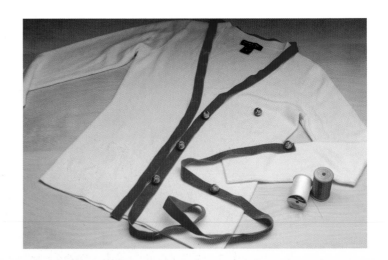

AFTER

## instructions

1. Start by finding the center front. Fold the sweater by matching and pinning the side seams together. With a needle and thread, thread-trace along the folded line at the center front (A), only through the sweater front. Open the sweater and lay it flat on a table. Slip a ruler or cardboard strip between the front and back sweater to create a surface on which to pin.

2. The nap or pile in velvet is directional. Hold it one way and it looks light (the nap is going down); the reverse looks dark (the nap is going up). Place the ribbon, right side up, along the right front (also right side up) with the nap going up. Begin with the ribbon ¼" (6 mm) below the center front hem (the bottom of the ribbing). Smooth the ribbon and pin it to the edge, or along one side of the thread tracing up toward the neck, slightly easing the ribbon's inside edge and stretching the outside edge of the ribbon along the neck edge. The inside edge of ribbon should line up with the center thread line, curve away from the thread line near the V point, and blend into the original neckline leading up to the shoulder.

3. Cut the ribbon so that it extends ¼" (6 mm) past the center back point on the neck edge. Repeat this process to attach ribbon on the left side of the sweater, making sure that the nap of the velvet is running in the same direction on both sides. Overlap the velvet at the back of the neck.

4. Carefully hand baste the ribbon in place close to each edge. Turn the sweater inside out. Adjust the needle position for precisely stitching the edge of the ribbon. Set your sewing machine for a stretch or narrow zigzag stitch. Sew the ribbon in place, starting at the back of the neck (B and C). Don't sew the ¼" (6 mm) extensions at center back.

5. Stitching toward the hem, puddle the sweater around the area being stitched. Imagine you are sewing the inside of a tube. Pull the excess fabric out of the way as you stitch (D).

6. End each row of machine stitching with backstitching. Trim the ribbon ends flush with the hem edge.

7. Start cutting from the hem, going up the center front between the ribbons (E). Cut along the ribbon edge to the neckline. Trim off the small wedge of sweater at the base of the V-neck. At center back, overlap and machine sew the ribbon extensions in place.

8. Divide the sleeve circumference into quarters. On the back quarter line (not the seamline) thread-trace a 7" (17.8 cm) -long line. This is where a placket is usually positioned on a shirt. Place a ruler or cardboard strip inside the sleeve to create a surface on which to pin the ribbon in place. Cut a length of ribbon ¼" (6 mm) longer than the desired placket length of 6" (15.2 cm). At the thread tracing, pin the cut ribbon on the sleeve, both with the right sides up and with the nap in the right direction (F). Let the beginning of the ribbon extend ¼" (6 mm) beyond the bottom of the sleeve. Baste both edges of the ribbon to the sleeve.

   Turn the sleeve inside out to machine stitch the ribbon in place. Turn the sleeve right side out and cut off the excess ribbon at both ends of the stitching lines. In the same manner, make a faux placket on the remaining sleeve.

9. Try the sweater on to determine the placement of the faux pocket. Mark the location with pins. Mark the center front waistline for the hook and eye placements.

10. Cut a ribbon 3½" (8.9 cm) long for each of the breast pockets. Cut a piece of ribbon for each of the hip pockets, each one measuring 4½" (11.4 cm) long.

11. Sew ribbons to the sweater front for the breast and hip pockets. Center each hip pocket between the center front vertical ribbon and the side seam and 4½" (11.4 cm) up from the hem.

12. Stitch the hook-and-eye sets ½" (1.3 cm) apart at the waist. Recede them slightly from the edge so that they are invisible from the front (see page 18). Stitch the buttons to the top center of the ribbons.

## Tip

When stitching a trim onto a ready-made garment, it may be easier to open a parallel seam and close it back up when finished. In the case of sweaters such as this one, the seams are too fine to open.

A

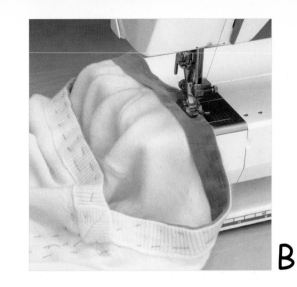

B

C

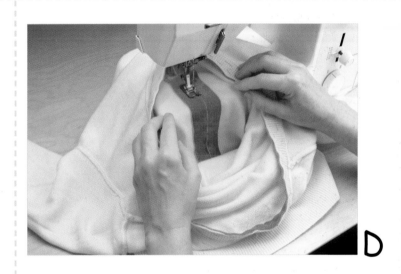

D

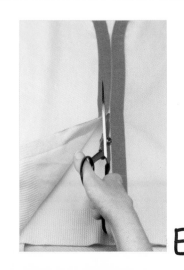

E

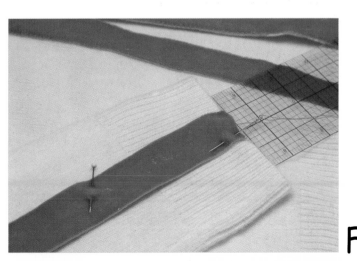

F

AFTER

# TIERED SKIRT TO STYLISH SUNDRESS

The tiered shape of this skirt is created with rows of elastic thread. Its length, though, is too long for someone under 5' 5" (165 cm) tall. A skirt with a ruffled or pleated hem must be shortened by cutting it off at the top. Here's how to turn a long skirt into a breezy sundress.

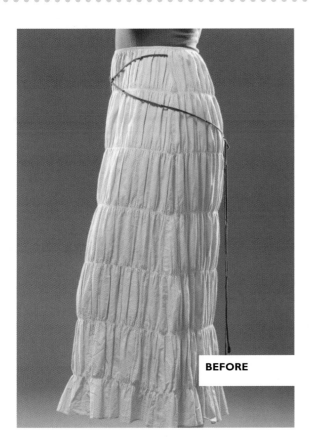

**BEFORE**

**LEVEL OF SKILL:** ★★

## materials

- basic sewing kit (see page 13)
- tiered skirt with gathered waist
- 2 yards (1.8 m) of 1¾" (4.5 cm) -wide galloon lace (scallops on both sides)
- sewing thread, color-matched to the fabric
- sewing thread, color-matched to the lace
- 7" (17.8 cm) long coil or invisible coil zipper
- 1 small hook-and-eye set
- rosebud leaf base pattern (see page 126)

Note: The finished dress fits loosely at the waist. If the skirt that you're transforming doesn't have a waist drawstring, you also need 3 yards (2.7 m) of strong decorative cord.

# instructions

**1.** Remove the tie belt from the side seams using a seam ripper. If the tie belt is inserted in a casing, just pull it out.

**2.** Pin the front and back of the skirt together along the gathering line of the top tier. Measure up 2" (5.1 cm) from the pinned line and chalk-mark a line parallel to the gathering line. Cut along the chalk line, through both fabric layers, to eliminate the elastic waistline (A). Do not discard it. (See Rosebud, page 24, for a suggestion on how to use it.)

**3.** Narrow hem the ruffle edge. To do this, first turn under the raw edge $\frac{3}{16}$" (4 mm). Baste the hem allowance (B). Now turn it under again and machine stitch the hem. (See page 18 for step-by-step instructions for a narrow hem.)

**4.** Measure your chest under the arms, above the bust. Add 2" (5.1 cm) to this measurement, for ease and a lace hem. Since the lace doesn't stretch, the left side seam of your skirt will need to be opened along the top 5" (12.7 cm) with a seam ripper. After opening the seam, baste the closed zipper in place so that the zipper head will be at the gathering line. Machine stitch the zipper in place (C). (See page 16 for step-by-step instructions to insert a zipper.)

**5.** Insert the tie belt ends into the side seams at the second gathering line, which will be under the bust. If your skirt didn't have a tie belt, cut the length of decorative cord in half and insert one end of each length into the side seam as previously noted. Sew the ends into the side seams.

**6.** Cut the lace to the final measurement that you obtained in step 4. Ignoring $\frac{1}{2}$" (1.3 cm) at both ends, which will be seam allowances later, divide the lace into quarters and mark each quarter (the center front, center back, and both side seams) with a pin or chalk mark. Find the center front and center back along the top gathering line. Mark each position with a pin. Centered on the uppermost gathering line, pin a short end of the lace to a side seam, leaving $\frac{1}{2}$" (1.3 cm) extending beyond the seam, to turn under along the side edge of the zipper (D).

Center the length of the lace over the top gathering line. Match and pin two of the lace quarter marks to the center front and center back on the dress. Evenly distribute the fullness of the dress along the gathering line to fit the lace. Pin, and then hand stitch the long edges of the lace in place. Use two rows of stitching spaced at least $\frac{1}{4}$" (6 mm) apart. Turn the short lace ends under and hand stitch them along the zipper. Attach a hook and eye above the top of the zipper.

**7.** Try on the dress. Measure over a shoulder, from the top gathering line in the front to the same gathering line in the back. Add 2" (5.1 cm) to this measurement, for the length to cut the lace for the shoulder straps. You need $\frac{1}{2}$" (13 mm) for each seam allowance and 1" (2.5 cm) for length adjustments at the back. Cut two lace straps, both the same length as the final measurement. Pin the straps to the dress and hand stitch them in place (E). Stitch two rows for strength.

## Tips

- Zipper lengths can be easily shortened by taking several satin stitches across the coil at the bottom of the desired length. Leave $\frac{1}{2}$" (1.3 cm) extending below the stitches and cut off the excess, using pinking shears. Don't try to shorten a zipper that has metal teeth.

- Hook-and-eye sets, spaced close together, could be used in place of a zipper for the side opening on this dress.

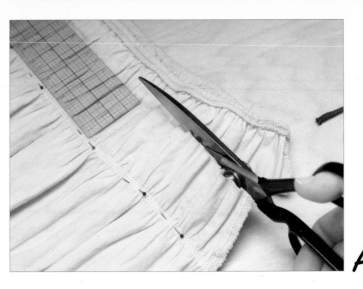

A

B

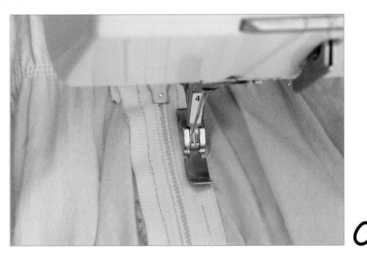

C

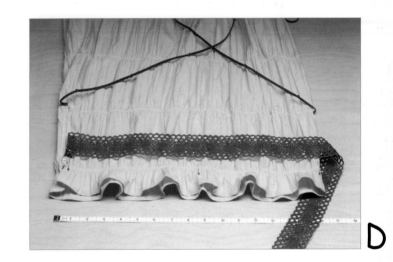

D

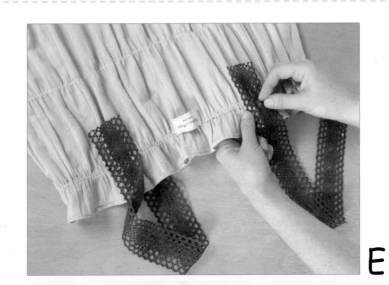

E

# SHAPELESS T-SHIRT TO SHOELACE TREASURE

With a knit remnant and an early '70s pattern, this hand-made T-shirt turned out too large. Rather than altering the side seams, which would involve redoing the hem, it was slimmed down with an empire-height drawstring. The added eyelets are both decorative and functional. No machine sewing required!

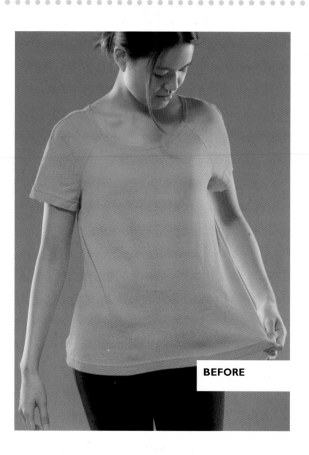

BEFORE

**LEVEL OF SKILL:** ★

## materials

- basic sewing kit (see page 13)
- loose T-shirt
- ¼ yard (0.2 m) of fusible tricot (knit) interfacing
- 3 yards (2.7 m) of ³⁄₁₆" (4 mm) -wide braid
- cotton sewing thread, any color
- 60 small eyelets
- awl or hole punch
- clear or masking tape
- wide ruler or strip of cardboard
- eyelet pliers

AFTER

## instructions

1. To mark the center front, fold the T-shirt, matching and pinning the side seams together. Trace along the folded line of the center front with a needle and thread, sewing through only the front layer. Standing in front of a mirror, try on the top and pin a line below the bust where the drawstring/waistline will be comfortable.

2. Turn the top inside out and lay it flat on a table. Slip a wide ruler or cardboard strip between the front and back of the shirt to create a surface on which to pin. Measure up from the bottom, across the entire front, to straighten and mark the new waistline with a line of pins. Continue the line around to the back. Draw the line with chalk and then thread-trace the line. Use an uneven hand basting stitch with a small stitch on the wrong side and a large stitch on the right side. This long-short stitch makes it easier to pull the thread out from underneath the fused interfacing that's applied in a later step.

3. Cut a strip of fusible interfacing 1¼" (3.2 cm) wide and as long as the T-shirt's circumference, to reinforce the fabric where the eyelets will be placed (along the new waistline) (A). Center the strip over the thread line, on the wrong side of the fabric, and press it in place (B).

4. Pin-mark the position of the eyelets at 2" (5.1 cm) intervals along the waistline. Begin at the center front and measure 1" (2.5 cm) on either side of the center front line. An eyelet will be placed at each of these two spots. Around the front and back of the shirt waistline, you can put in as many eyelets as you want, as long as the total amount is an even number. Turn the T-shirt right side out. Mark dots with a chalk pencil on the right side at each pin-mark.

5. On a scrap of fabric that has a piece of interfacing fused to the back, make a practice sample eyelet, following the instructions that follow.

6. Punch a hole in the fabric with an awl. Make sure the hole is large enough for the eyelet placed on the eyelet pliers but not too large that the eyelet will pull out.

7. This technique can be tricky to do in the center of a garment such as the waist because of all the fabric in the way. Place the eyelet pliers at the shortest distance from the eyelet site (through the armhole in some cases) (C). Be careful to pull the excess fabric out of the way. Continue applying the eyelet by following the instructions in the kit.

8. Cut a 2-yard (1.82 m) length of braid. Wrap a small piece of tape tightly around the braid end to prevent it from fraying. Weave the braid in and out of the eyelets, beginning and ending at center front (D). Pull the cord through. Trim and knot the ends.

9. Position eyelets around the neckline at 1" (2.5 cm) intervals. If the neckline already has a faced or hemmed edge, no fusible interfacing is needed. Cut a 28" (71.1 cm) length of braid and lace it through the eyelets around the neck. The ends can be trimmed, overlapped, and hand stitched in place on the inside of the center back neck. Remove all of the basting threads.

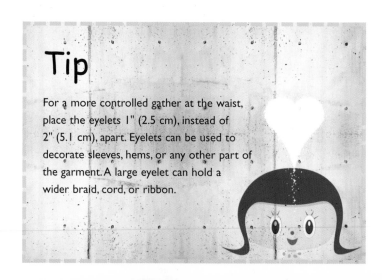

## Tip

For a more controlled gather at the waist, place the eyelets 1" (2.5 cm), instead of 2" (5.1 cm), apart. Eyelets can be used to decorate sleeves, hems, or any other part of the garment. A large eyelet can hold a wider braid, cord, or ribbon.

A

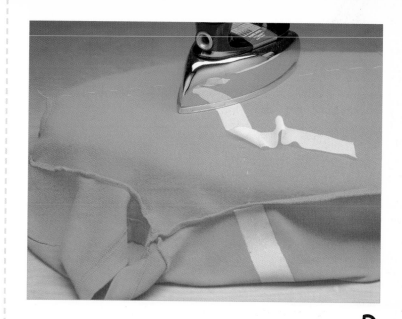

B

C

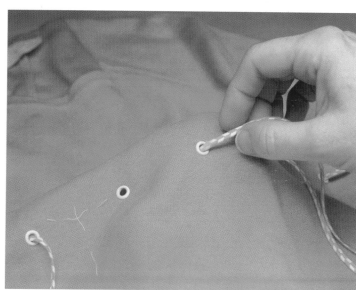

D

AFTER

# HIS POLO TO HER POLYNESIA

This shirt was probably a Father's Day gift never worn. With its hangtag still attached, the distinctive print stood out on a thrift store rack. An easy summer skirt came to mind. The sleeves were removed and turned upside down to become pockets. An elasticized waist and rope belt completed the look, or so I thought. My husband asked why I had not used the scraps to make a top. Cut off the back and collar and presto—you have a halter to match!

**BEFORE**

**LEVEL OF SKILL:** ★★

## materials

- basic sewing kit (see page 13)
- polo shirt, men's large or extra large
- 1 yard (0.9 m) of 1" (25 mm) no-roll elastic
- 6 yards (5.5 m) of cord or rope ³⁄₁₆" (4.7 mm) in diameter for the belt
- 2 yards (1.8 m) of cord or rope ⁵⁄₁₆" (8 mm) in diameter for the top
- sewing thread, color-matched to the garment
- ¼ yard (0.2 m) of ½" (13 mm) -wide single fold bias tape
- ½ yard (0.5 m) of ⅞" (22 mm) -wide single fold bias tape
- 2 tassels
- 18 wood beads with holes large enough for cord or rope
- large binder clip
- loop turner or small safety pin
- 3 rubber bands
- masking tape
- fabric glue
- polo top pattern (see page 129)

## instructions

1. Mark a straight line with chalk just below the armhole. Cut off along this line, and save the bottom for the skirt (A).

2. Cut off the sleeves. Keep one folded. Chalk an 8½" (21.6 cm) -long line parallel to the lengthwise grain, starting at the hemline of the sleeve ribbing. At the far end of the chalked line, chalk a line that's 7" (17.8 cm) long and square to the first line. Slash along the fold and cut along the chalked lines (B). You have cut out two pockets from one sleeve. The ribbed hem finish will be the top of the pocket.

3. Turn and baste under ¼" (6 mm) along the side and bottom edges of both pockets (C). Place each pocket on the front, 4½" (11.4 cm) down from the waist (the upper, cut edge) and 1½" (3.8 cm) in from a side seam. Pin, baste, and edgestitch the pockets in place (D).

4. Using the leftover fabric from the shirt (above the first cut line that ran across the armhole), measure a 2¾" (7 cm) -wide waistband and cut off from the bottom of the remaining polo shirt (between the armholes and below the button placket) for the front and back waistband. For the waistband length, take your measurement around the fullest area of your hips and subtract 1" (2.5 cm). The waistband should be long enough to stretch over your hips. Add a ¼" (6 mm) -wide seam allowance at each side seam (short edge), and sew the short ends together to make a circle (E). Finish one long edge of the waistband with a zigzag or overlock serger stitch.

5. Mark the center front and center back on the waistband and skirt with small scissor clips in the seam allowances. Gather the top of the skirt with two rows of large machine stitches and adjust the skirt to fit the waistband by pulling the bobbin threads. Don't attach the waistband yet.

6. Cut a 1¼" x 18" (3.2 X 45.7 cm) strip of fabric for belt carriers. Fold the strip and stitch the long edges together using a ¼" (6 mm) -wide seam allowance. Turn the strip right side out with a loop turner or small safety pin attached to one end and pushed through, to a finished ⅜" (1 cm) width. Cut the strip into five pieces, each 3½" (8.9 cm) long. At the waistband seam, pin a short end of one strip at the center back, one near each side seam and two equally spaced along the front, where you would see princess lines on a woman's shirt. Baste the strips in place with a short raw end in the seam allowance.

7. Pin and machine stitch the waistband to the skirt matching the center front and center back clips (F). Fold over the waistband so that it's 1" (2.5 cm) deep, to allow room for the 1" (25 mm) -wide elastic. Let the extra waistband fabric extend past the waist seam on the inside of the skirt and stitch in the ditch (see page 23) of the waistband seamline. Leave the waistband open 1½" (3.8 cm) at the center back for the elastic entrance.

# Tips

• Classic men's polo shirts come in a variety of colors. Mix and match by using sleeves of one color for pockets on a skirt of another color.

• Use the three-button placket for the top to contrast or match the pocket on the skirt.

• A complementary patterned men's tie could work as a belt.

A

B

C

D

E

belt carrier

F

**8.** Cut elastic to the measurement of the high hip (3" or 7.6 cm, down from the waist) minus 1" (2.5 cm). Pin a large safety pin on one end of the elastic and guide it through the waistband (G). Join the elastic ends by overlapping ½" (1.3 cm). Secure with hand or machine stitches. Stitch the waistband opening closed.

**9.** Fold under the raw edge of each belt carrier and stitch it in place at the top of the waistband.

**10.** Cut off 1½ yards (1.37 m) of the cord and reserve it for the bra top. Divide and cut the remaining cord into thirds. Use a large binder clip to secure the lengths together at one end. Bundle the opposite end of each length with a rubber band. Let out the bundle as needed while braiding the belt. Knot the strands together to hold the braid, leaving 10" (25.4 cm) unbraided for the belt ends (H). Tightly tape the cord ends so that it's easier to slip them through the beads. Space the beads out by placing knots between them. Attach a tassel to a loose strand at each end by threading a tassel loop through two beads and knotting it to the belt end. Remove the tape. A drop of fabric glue will seal the cord ends and prevent fraying.

**11.** For the halter top (I), cut off the collar along the neckline seam and the back along the shoulder seam. Use the pattern (see page 135) as a template for shaping the top and sides of the bra. (The pattern fits an A or B cup.)

**12.** Finish each armhole with ½" (1.3 cm) -wide bias tape by unfolding one long edge and seaming it to the right side along the tape's fold line. Let the tape ends extend a bit past the fabric edge, and fold this to the inside. Turn the tape to the inside along the seamline and topstitch it ⅜" (1 cm) from the edge.

**13.** Staystitch along the bottom edge. Gather where indicated to 2½" (6.4 cm), for fullness under the bust. Stitch the wide bias tape to the shoulder and bottom of the top, in the same manner that you attached tape to the armholes. Don't fold it to the inside yet.

**14.** Cut 20" (50.8 cm) of cord for the halter strap. Knot and place one end inside the bias tape at one shoulder. Fold the tape over the cord and hand stitch the folded edge to the seamline, forming a casing for the cord. Slide the bias binding down over the cord to form gathers. Repeat for the other side.

**15.** Cut two lengths of cord, each 15" (38.1 cm) long. Hand stitch the ends to the points indicated on the pattern. Fold the bias tape up and stitch the folded edge to the seamline, forming a bound hem. Some of the bias tape will be visible on the outside of the top. Knot the cord ends (J).

## Tips

Stitching a label into the center back waist makes getting dressed easier.

Make your own labels with a ribbon and a permanent marking pen.

G

H

I

J

# FLAT '50s FROCK TO FLIRTY FABULOUS DRESS

Found at an antiques booth at a state fair, the embroidered bodice and finely gathered skirt on this dress was too pretty to pass up. Yet, the roll-up sleeves were too sporty and the skirt was flat. A long, pink tulle skirt was adapted for a crinoline to bring the skirt to life.

**BEFORE**

## LEVEL OF SKILL: ★★★

### materials

- basic sewing kit (see page 13)
- dress or skirt and top with embroidered bodice and a gathered skirt
- crinoline or half slip
- 2 yards (1.8 m) of 58" (1.5 m) -wide tulle in a matching or contrasting color for the crinoline
- 1½ yards (1.4 m) of single fold bias binding tape, color-matched to the bodice
- 1 yard (0.9 m) of 1" (25 mm) -wide grosgrain ribbon, color-matched to the skirt (optional, for a new waistband)
- 12" (30.5 cm) of ¼" (6 mm) -wide twill tape, color-matched to the bodice
- 2 pieces of felt, each 2" (5.1 cm) × waist measurement (see step 8), color-matched to the bodice
- fusible web 2" (5.1 cm) × waist measurement
- 1 spool of topstitching thread or 2 spools of sewing thread to match the embroidery
- sewing thread, color-matched to the garments
- 4" (10.2 cm) of boning or rigilene
- 4 yards (3.6 m) total of narrow ribbon or cord
- 4 eyelets
- trouser hook and eye (optional, for a new crinoline waistband)

Note: Single-fold bias tape could be used for a casing around the boning or rigilene to do a really nice job.

AFTER

## instructions

1. Using a seam ripper, remove the sleeves from the armhole. Detach the neckline facing where it's tacked down to the shoulder seam allowance.

2. To gather the shoulder, cut a piece of bias binding the length of the shoulder seam. Center the tape over the seamline, and stitch one side of the bias binding to only one side of one of the seam allowances (not through to the right side of the bodice) (A).

3. Attach the twill tape by hand or machine at the neckline, placing it inside the bias tape (between the bias tape and the open seam allowances). Stitch the loose side of the bias tape to the other seam allowance.

4. Pull the loose end of the twill tape at the armhole end to gather the shoulder as much as you want. Adjust and stitch the twill tape end at the armhole. Make sure each shoulder seam finishes at the same length, which is 3" to 4" (7.6 to 10.2 cm). Tack the neck facing back down at the shoulder seam.

5. If there is a side zipper on the bodice, it will need to be picked out to the waist. Take in the side seams ½" (1.3 cm) at the armhole and taper to nothing at the waist (B). Trim the seam allowances to ½" (1.3 cm). Sew the zipper back in place.

6. To finish the armhole, open one lengthwise fold of the bias tape and fold the short end under ¼" (6 mm) and pin it at the side seam. Ease and pin the unfolded edge of the tape around the armhole, with the right sides together. Machine stitch ¼" (6 mm) from the edge (C). Clip seam allowance and turn the tape to the inside of the armhole and stitch the tape down. This can be held in place with topstitching ⅜" (1 cm) from the seam or with an invisible hand stitch.

7. Measure around your waist and subtract 1" (2.5 cm) (D). This is the finished length of the belt.

8. Cut two pieces of felt and one piece of fusible web 2" (5.1 cm) wide by the finished belt length. Sandwich the web between the felt pieces and fuse the layers together with an iron.

9. Make a sample of decorative stitches to decide which to use for decorating the belt. Adjust the stitch length to 4 or 5 (6 or 8 spi). Machine straight stitch ¼" (6 mm) in from all edges of the belt edge by using a topstitching thread or two spools of all-purpose thread that are fed together through the machine needle. Begin stitching at the center back of the belt. Use the presser foot as a guide for stitching the lines. Inside the straight stitch, along all edges and turning the corners, place your decorative stitch (E). Pull thread ends through to the wrong side and knot them.

10. Place two evenly spaced sets of eyelets ½" (1.3 cm) in from each end of the belt. On the inside of the belt, cut and catch stitch a piece of boning between the eyelets and the edges, parallel to the short edges, to keep the belt ends firm. Cut and loop 1 yard (0.9 m) ribbon pieces halfway through each eyelet, and knot the lengths together close to the belt ends (F).

11. Adjust the waist of the crinoline to fit snugly around the waist and high hip area. (Try on the garment, pin out the excess, from the waist to the high hip, chalk new seamlines, and then stitch along the chalk lines. Open the old seam, and trim the seam allowances.) Using the matching tulle, cut six panels, each 12" (30.5 cm) wide and the full width of the tulle. Unfolded, each panel is 12" X 58" (30.5 X 147.3 cm). Gather one cut edge of each panel with two rows of long (3 mm or 9 spi) stitches (see page 16).

12. On the inside of the crinoline, chalk a line 4" (10.2 cm) down from the waist. Cut one of the panels in half through the width. Join two and one-half panels end-to-end to make a circle. Stitch the tulle to the chalked line, around the entire skirt circumference.

13. Join and stitch three and one-half panels to the hem of the first ruffled tier. The hem is left as a cut edge.

## Tips

• These instructions and materials will make one crinoline layer. Add as many tulle layers as you wish. Different colors can be used—as shown in the photo on page 73.

• If the waistline of your crinoline has no zipper, just stay stitch around the opening. Finish the waist with a ribbon waistband and hook-and-eye as shown on page 116 (H).

A

B

C

D

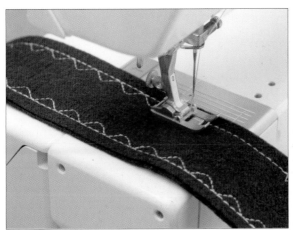

E

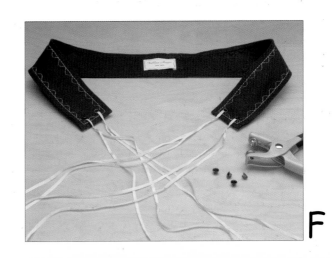

F

AFTER

# SIMPLE STRAPLESS TO BODICE BEAUTY

Without its original belt, this dress was in desperate need of definition. The solution mixes a stripe with a floral print for a stylish spin on a summer standard. Partner classic elements from a tailored cotton shirt to create unique bodice details. The cuffs are appliquéd to the center front for a tux shirt look. The body of the shirt provides the sash belt and the front button placket becomes a halter strap, which cleverly buttons onto the cuffs.

**BEFORE**

**LEVEL OF SKILL:** ★★

## materials
- basic sewing kit (see page 13)
- strapless dress with waistline seam
- striped shirt
- sewing thread, color-matched to the shirt

## instructions

1. The dress shown in the step-by-step photos has a waistline seam. If your dress doesn't have one, try it on and pin-mark the waist location only on the front. Take off the dress and thread-trace the waistline on the dress front. Remove the pins. Fold the top to match the side seams from the top to the waist. Pin and then thread-trace a center front line on the dress bodice.

2. Cut the cuffs off the shirt along the seamlines (A). If desired, machine embroider along the cuffs. Place a cuff on either side of the center thread tracing, with the cuff button at the top on opposite sides. Align the button edge of each cuff with the top, horizontal edge of the bodice. If the cuffs are too wide for the bib front, turn each cut edge under and slightly taper the cuff width toward the waist for a narrower look. On both pieces, the end of the cuff that has the buttonhole is at the waist. Turn under this end on both pieces, hiding each button-hole. If the cuff ends extend quite a bit past the bodice waist-line, just trim off some of the excess and then pin the rest under. Press and pin the edges in place.

3. Cut a 7" (17.8 cm) -wide sash from the back of the shirt at its longest point (from the shoulder to the hem). If the fabric has an uneven stripe pattern and a visible right and wrong side, cut a left and right sash that mirror one another. The front shirt can also be used for the sash. If needed, add extra length by trimming the sash ends on the diagonal and adding an extra strip, cut on the crosswise grain, and used it to face the ends. The finished length of each sash is 29" (72.4 cm).

4. Narrow hem the long edges of the sash by pressing the seam allowance under a scant (a little less than) ¼" (6 mm) then another ¼" (6 mm) (B).

5. Stitch the pressed hem close to the folded edge (C).

6. Gather the straight ends of the sash with two rows of long stitching, spaced about ¼" (6 mm) apart, to achieve a finished sash width of 2¼" (5.7 cm). Tuck and pin the gathered ends ½" (1.3 cm) under the outer cuff edges, at the waistline (D). Edgestitch the outer edges of the cuffs to the bodice front. Fold back ½" (1.3 cm) of the cuff edges along the center front line and blind hem stitch the edges in place.

7. On the shirt front, mark a ½" (1.3 cm) seam allowance along the button placket and cut the placket off the shirt along this line. This placket will be the halter strap. Press the seam allowance under ¼" (6 mm), turn to the wrong side of the placket and slipstitch in place.

8. Try on the dress to measure the length of the halter strap, which is one piece that wraps around the neck and buttons onto the top of the cuff. Turn, hem, and make an extra button-hole on the strap, if necessary, for a perfect fit. Remove the unused shirt buttons, space, and then stitch, them evenly along the cuff edge for a decorative finish (E).

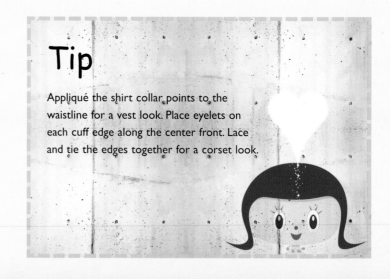

## Tip

Appliqué the shirt collar points to the waistline for a vest look. Place eyelets on each cuff edge along the center front. Lace and tie the edges together for a corset look.

A

B

C

D

E

# OFFICE CARDIGAN TO CROPPED TOPPER

Even petite-sized sweaters seemed to swim on my student, Sarah. She customizes them by cutting out a section below the bust to shorten them while retaining the delicate hem finish. This project uses her technique on a thrift store sweater. A ribbon covers the cut line and a purchased beaded appliqué make it the perfect cool evening cover-up for sleeveless styles.

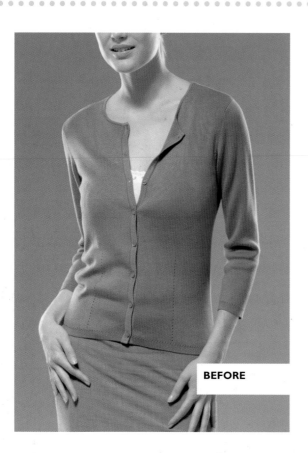

**BEFORE**

**LEVEL OF SKILL:** ☆

## materials

- basic sewing kit (see page 13)
- fine-knit cardigan
- ¼ yard (0.2 m) fusible tricot (knit) interfacing
- 2½ yards (2.3 m) of ⅝" (16 mm) velvet stretch ribbon
- square of nonwoven medium-weight interfacing slightly larger than the appliqué
- sewing thread, color-matched to the garment
- sewing thread, color-matched to the appliqué
- 1 beaded appliqué

Note: Wrap a scrap of ribbon or twill tape around your underbust and make a bow. Now take it off and measure the length, adding twice the length needed for the bow. Compare this to the stretch ribbon yardage specified to make sure that you're buying enough.

AFTER

## instructions

1. To shorten the sweater, try it on and pin a twill tape below the bust. Make sure the twill tape is level all the way around your body. Remove the cardigan, lay it flat, and pin a second line 3" (7.6 cm) down from the first line (A). Mark a chalk line along both pieces of the twill tape and thread-trace along the chalk lines, with short stitches in the wrong side and long stitches on the right side.

2. Cut 1½" (3.8 cm) -wide strips of interfacing on the crosswise grain. (Cut on this grain; the interfacing will have a bit of stretch.) You'll need enough strips to wrap around the entire cardigan at both of the thread-traced lines. These will stabilize the knit while cutting the cardigan.

3. Place strips of interfacing centered over the thread-traced style lines, on the wrong side of the cardigan, and fuse them in place with a dry iron (no steam) (B). If your cardigan doesn't have tightly knit or fabric-faced front plackets, make sure that interfacing strips cover the thread-traced area of the plackets.

4. Add a ½" (1.3 cm) seam allowance to the inside of the style lines and cut out the center section along the seam allowance lines. You can cut the sweater on the double if you align the hem and pin together the front edges (C).

5. Overlap and pin the hem section over the upper cardigan, matching the thread-traced lines (D). Hand stitch through all the layers. Try on the sweater to check the hem length and make any adjustments necessary. Machine stitch the layers together along the matched thread-traced lines (E). Trim the seam allowances down to ¼" (6 mm) on both sides.

6. Center the ribbon over the stitching line. Pin the midpoint of the ribbon length at the center back and continue pinning it to the cardigan toward both of the fronts (F). To create a double-faced tie, you want to have velvet facing out on both sides of each ribbon tie that extends past the cardigan's front edge. At the desired tie length, fold the ribbon across the width and pin the excess ribbon back on itself, ending at the center front. Repeat for the other tie.

7. Edgestitch the ribbon in place, starting on the top edge at the center back and moving out to the folded ends. Backstitch and repeat for the lower edge of the ribbon (G). Also sew together the long edges of the ribbon that extend past center front.

8. Cut a piece of the fusible interfacing slightly larger than the appliqué. Decide the appliqué placement on the garment, and fuse the interfacing to the wrong side of the cardigan, as a stabilizer. Pin the appliqué on the right side of the cardigan and hand stitch it in place using a tiny running stitch just inside the outer row of beads (H).

## Tips

• If you piece lengths of interfacing for step 3, the ends should butt together rather than overlap.

• If you sew with polyester sewing thread, you probably don't have to worry about stitches breaking as the stretchy sweater fabric shifts. If using other sewing thread, straight stitch the seam, hold both ends, and snap the seam, and then straight stitch it again. Or just use a very narrow zigzag stitch.

• Hand stitch a strip of lace inside the cardigan, at the waist, to cover the seam.

• Create your signature cardigan by substituting the appliqué for embroidery, beading, or a fabric flower.

A

B

C

D

E

F

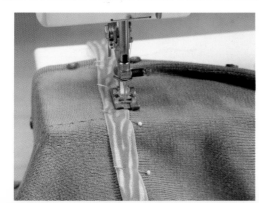

G

H

AFTER

# PLAIN-JANE JACKET TO KNIT-AND-NYLON EYE-CATCHER

This 1971 college field hockey jacket had not been worn in years. Inspired by stylish athlethic-wear designs, its proportions are transformed by combining the lower half of a ribbed knit cardigan with the top half of the jacket. The finished product is an exaggerated baseball-style jacket, perfect for post-workout gallivanting.

**BEFORE**

**LEVEL OF SKILL:** ★★★

## materials
- basic sewing kit (see page 13)
- sports team jacket
- collar pattern (see page 126)
- 1 medium- to heavyweight ribbed knit pullover or cardigan
- sewing thread, color-matched to the jacket

## instructions

1. Lay the front of the jacket flat and face up on a table. Fold the cardigan along center front and lay the cardigan over half the jacket, to determine the proportions. Mark the hemline on the jacket 1" (2.5 cm) below the last snap by pinning twill tape across the front, parallel to the existing hemline (A). Pin a second length of twill tape ½" (1.3 cm) above the pockets (A) and extend that line across the entire back.

   To create a front placket that extends to the hemline, pin a line 1¾" (4.5 cm) away from—and parallel to—the vertical center front opening (A). Use a ruler to mark all of the lines with chalk. Remove the tape after making the chalk lines. Remember to also chalk the lines on the back of the body and the back of the sleeves.

2. Measure up from the jacket sleeve hem 6½" (16.5 cm) and pin a tape line perpendicular to the center grain or fold line along the top of the sleeve, not the underarm seamline (A). If the sleeve is tapered (not just gathered at the wrist) make sure the tape line is always the same distance from the sleeve hem. Measure up from the cardigan sleeve hem 7½" (19.1 cm) and mark a tape line (A). Mark these lines with chalk, and then remove the tape.

3. Add a ½" (1.3 cm) seam allowance above the marked lines on the cardigan. Add a ½" (1.3 cm) seam allowance below and outside the marked lines on the jacket. Add 1" (2.5 cm) for the hem of the center front placket. Mark these lines with chalk and then remove the tape.

4. Pin and baste along the jacket cut lines to hold layers (lining, facings) together.

5. Cut away the jacket body and sleeves above the hems, at the closest chalk lines (B). Cut off the cardigan hem and sleeve cuffs at the upper chalk lines (B). Before cutting, you might want to hand baste the jacket lining to the outer shell. This will prevent the lining from slipping or twisting. Remove the collar from the jacket neckline with a seam ripper (B).

6. Cut a rectangle 4" (10.2 cm) along the lengthwise rib and 15" (38.1 cm) across the back of the cardigan (B and C). Using the sweater rectangle and collar pattern on page 126, cut out a new jacket collar (B).

7. Machine staystitch ⅜" (1 cm) in from the cut edges of the jacket (D).

8. Clip diagonally into the front placket corner for ease in joining it to the rib knit (E). Do not cut deeper than ½" (1.3 cm).

## Tip

If you are using an oversized jacket, the collar might be too short to fit the neckline. Use a tape measure to measure around the jacket neckline from the center front to the center back (do not include the center front extension). Adjust the collar by splitting the pattern at the center back line adding the difference to each side.

A

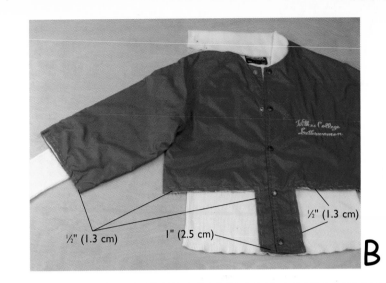

½" (1.3 cm)          1" (2.5 cm)          ½" (1.3 cm)

B

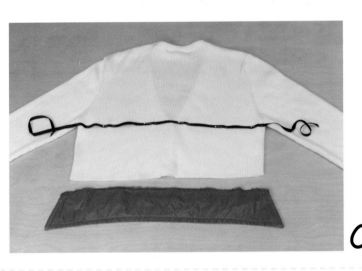

C

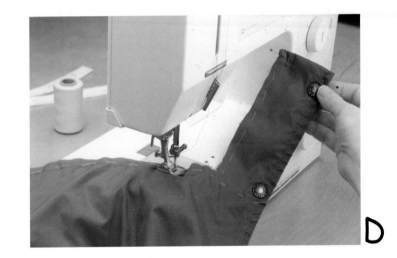

D

E

**9.** Hem both of the center front jacket plackets by turning each edge under ⅜" (1 cm) and again ⅝" (1.6 cm). Machine stitch across each hem.

**10.** Cut off the cardigan placket. The distance around the horizontal cut edge of the rib cardigan hem should measure a little more than two-thirds of the distance around the cutoff jacket hem (front, back, and front).

**11.** The upper edge of the rib should be set in evenly around the jacket hem. Divide and mark the back of both the jacket and rib into quarters between the side seams. Mark the ribbing with chalk or tiny V-clips no deeper than ⅜" (1 cm). Divide the front of the jacket between the side seams and placket into halves and mark in the same manner. Also divide and mark the front of the rib between the side seams and the rib ends into halves. With the wrong sides together and using a ½" (1.3 cm) seam allowance, baste, and then machine stitch, the vertical rib ends to the placket of the jacket, perfectly matching the lower, finished edge (hem) of the rib with the placket hem.

**12.** Pin the side seam of the rib to the side seam of the jacket hem at the upper edge of the cardigan. Stretch and match the rest of the ribbing marks to the jacket marks, pinning the

wrong sides together (F). Machine stitch the rib to the jacket. Finish the seam edges with zigzag or overlock stitches.

**13.** Turn the seam allowance up, toward the neck, and topstitch ¼" (6 mm) from the seam, on the right side (G).

**14.** Divide the jacket sleeve and the rib cuff into quarters. Mark, stretch, and pin the cuff to the jacket sleeve with the wrong sides together. Machine stitch, finish the edges with zigzag or overlock stitches, and topstitch with the seam allowances turned up toward the sleeve cap (H).

**15.** At the neck edge, fold the jacket lining away from the shell. Staystitch the jacket neck. Fold the rib collar in half lengthwise and hand baste the cut edges together. Mark the center back of the jacket neckline and the collar with a pin or tiny V-clip. Match and pin each side of the collar from the center back to the center front. If the original collar didn't extend across the top of the placket, don't attach the new collar there, because the edge is already finished (I). Baste, and then machine stitch, the collar to the right side of the jacket shell neck only. Clip the seam allowances. Hand slipstitch the facing or lining along the neckline to finish the inside of the jacket. Topstitch ¼" (6 mm) from the seamline, on the jacket side.

## Tip

Make or purchase a fun appliqué to stitch above the existing logo or on the back of the jacket.

F

G

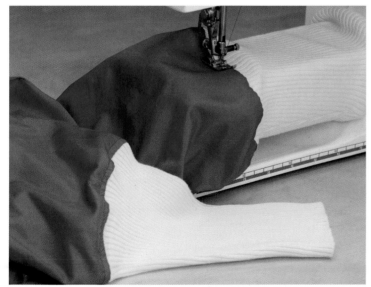

H

I

# STRETCHED-OUT TEE TO SPARKLING HALTER

Bare shoulders lend an elegant, evening look in rich fabrics such as velvet. Reconstruction on this garment is simple since the fabric has stretch. Vintage metallic braid from the '60s gave it the perfect finish.

**BEFORE**

**LEVEL OF SKILL:** ★★

## materials

- basic sewing kit (see page 13)
- mock turtleneck stretch velvet top
- 3 yards (2.7 m) of 1½" (3.8 cm) -wide metallic braid
- ½ yard (0.5 m) fusible tricot (knit) interfacing
- sewing thread, color-matched to the garment
- sewing thread, color-matched to the trim
- 12" (30.5 cm) of 1" (25 mm) -wide grosgrain ribbon
- 4 hook-and-eye sets
- 2 snaps
- 1 yard (0.9 m) of ¼" (6 mm) -wide ribbon or twill tape
- carbon paper, in a color that contrasts with the top fabric (optional, see step 4)
- thick towel

Note: Choose a braid that won't scratch your skin.

AFTER

## instructions

1. Turn the top inside out and pin the side seams together. Fold the top in half to find the center back. Chalk-mark and then thread-trace along the center back, stitching through only a single layer.

2. Measure down from each of the shoulder seams 1¼" (3.2 cm) along the front neckline and mark each spot with a pin. Try the top on with a strapless bra and stand in front of a mirror to pin the style line. Pin a slightly diagonal line with twill tape starting at the neckline pin-mark point, traveling down the chest, and curving over to the armhole/side seam (A). With the help of a friend or on a dress form, continue pinning around to the center back with the twill tape just above the bra line. It's only necessary to pin the line on one side of the back.

3. Pin out the excess fullness the same amount at both of the side seams, from the underarm to the waist, tapering to nothing just above the hem. Repeat at the center back, shaping it in at the top, waist, and hem (B). This will become a seam. Avoid fitting the garment so tightly that it will be impossible to take off without a zipper opening. Mark along the pins with chalk.

4. Take the top off and lay it flat. Draw a chalk line to smooth and correct the style and seamlines. Thread-trace along the chalked lines (C). Transfer the halter style line to the other side of the back using carbon paper or tailor's tacks, then thread-trace these lines (D). Cut the top open along the center back and use a seam ripper to open the collar seam (at the center back).

5. Cut four strips of interfacing on the lengthwise grain, each 1¾" × 12" (4.4 × 30.5 cm). Below the front neckline seam, pin a strip along a style line (inside and below the line). Ease around the armhole curve and cut off the excess at the side seam. Repeat for the remaining front and back style lines.

6. Cover the ironing board with a thick terrycloth towel. Turn off the steam setting on your iron. Lay the velvet pile face-down on the towel. Fuse the interfacing in place, placing the iron only where interfacing is being applied.

7. Machine staystitch along the upper edge of each interfacing strip. Cut the shirt along these lines and ¼" (6 mm) below the collar's neckline seam (E). Stitch the back closed along the two outermost thread tracing lines near the center back, leaving open 4" (10.2 cm) at the top, to form a placket.

8. Sew the side seams as pinned.

9. To achieve the best fit and shaping through the armhole area, pin the braid in place on the garment while it's on your body or a dress form. Pin the braid along a cut edge of the halter line starting ¼" (6 mm) above the neckline seam, down the front armhole, and around to the back. The outer braid edge should extend 1" (2.5 cm) past the cut edge of the garment.

10. From the wrong side, hand stitch the outer edge of the braid in place over the cut fabric edge using an overcast stitch (F). The inside edge of the braid can be stitched to the top from the right side with the same stitch (G). A flatter braid can be applied by machine, but baste it in place first.

11. Pin and sew another length of braid to the collar, hiding the ends of the first braid pieces underneath. Turn the excess fabric at the bottom of the collar and braid ends inside and hand stitch them in place. Lap the right side over the left in the back. Use strips of grosgrain ribbon to face each side of the center back placket opening. To create the placket opening, overlap the edges and then fold inside and hand tack the seam allowance on the upper layer. Stitch two hook-and-eye sets at the center back collar, and another two sets at the top of the placket. Add a snap inside the top and middle of the placket.

12. Pin and stitch a length of braid around the hem. Cut two lengths of ribbon or narrow twill tape, each 18" (45.7 cm) long. Fold one length in half across the width and stitch the ends together, inside the side seam for a hanger loop (H). Attach the remaining length to the other side seam in the same way.

## Tip

Avoid pressing velvet, even from the wrong side, unless you have the proper equipment. A needle board is ideal, but it's expensive. You can substitute a thick towel or use a steamer to eliminate wrinkles.

A

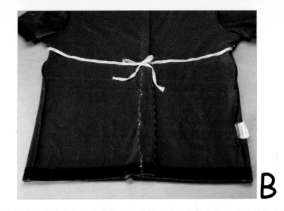

B

C

D

E

F

G

H

AFTER

# Dot Dress to Party Princess

Polka dots should bring to mind bubbles and parties and fun, so that became the theme for this makeover. Pretty but too serious, this dress morphed into a fantastic party frock.

The necktie was swathed in satin and shifted to the waistline. Flounces of tulle burst out from under a shortened skirt and add swing. Uncork the champagne!

BEFORE

**LEVEL OF SKILL: ★★★**

## materials

- basic sewing kit (see page 13)
- sleeveless, fully lined dress
- 2 yards (1.8 m) of 1½" (38 mm) -wide satin ribbon, in matching or contrasting color, for the belt
- ½ yard (0.5 m) of ½" (13 mm) -wide satin ribbon, color-matched to the dress for trimming the shoulder seam
- 2 hook-and-eye sets for the belt
- sewing thread, each one color-matched to the fabric
- sewing thread, color-matched to the ribbon
- sewing thread, color-matched to the tulle
- 1½" (3.8 cm) -wide strip of fusible web (see step 6 for the length)
- light- or medium-weight, woven fusible interfacing, 2" (5.1 cm) wide and the same length as the lining hem circumference
- 4 yards (3.6 m) of 70" (177.8 cm) -wide fine net tulle
- 4 yards (3.6 m) of 70" (177.8 cm) -wide fine net tulle in a second color

## instructions

1. Remove the tie from the neckline with a seam ripper. There may be up to three rows of stitches, so take your time and work under a bright light (A). Reserve the tie for use as a belt later.

2. This dress has a full lining that acts as a facing for the neck and armholes. In order to alter the fit of the dress, the lining will probably have to be released from the hemline, where it's most likely attached. Do this now.

3. To lower the front neckline, remove the remaining row of understitching that holds the seam allowance to the lining (or facing if the dress isn't lined) and then turn the dress inside out. The right side of the lining should be against the right side of the dress. Measure down 2½" (6.4 cm) from the point of the V-neck. Press a 1" (2.5 cm) square of fusible interfacing at the new neck point to reinforce it. Mark a new neckline with chalk, blending it into the original line as you draw toward the shoulders. Make sure that both sides of the new neckline blend in with the old around the same location. Machine stitch the dress and lining back together along the new neckline. Clip down to the V point, trim, and clip the seam allowances. Stitch the neckline closed where it was opened to release the tie. Turn the lining back to the inside of the dress and press the new neckline. It can be edgestitched for a quick finish.

4. To reduce the shoulder width, form two tucks at each shoulder seam, handling the lining and dress as a single layer and making each tuck ¼" (6 mm) deep. Fold the tucks flat, turned away from the neckline. Invisibly hand stitch each tuck 1" (2.5 cm) down on either side of the shoulder seam.

5. Cut two pieces of the ½" (13 mm) -wide ribbon, making the length of each piece twice the measurement of the new shoulder line plus 1" (2.5 cm). Center and secure one end of the ribbon on the inside shoulder seam. Wrap the ribbon around the right side and bring it back to the inside (B). Fold the ribbon end under, overlap the ends, and hand stitch them in place. Hand tack the band in place with a few tiny stitches on either end of the shoulder seam, on the wrong side.

6. To make a belt, tuck the seam allowance of the tie (that was joined to the neckline) inside of the tie. Press the folded edges and slipstitch them closed. Cut the 1½" (38 mm) ribbon 1" (2.5 cm) longer than the tie. Cut the fusible web to match the length of the tie and width of the ribbon. Use a rotary blade and self-healing cutting mat when cutting fusible out of yard goods for a perfect line. Two lengths of the ¾" (1.9 cm) -wide fusible web on a roll can be substituted for a strip cut from yardage (C).

7. Sandwich the fusible web between the ribbon and the tie. Turn under the ribbon ends to match the tie ends. Slip another, small, piece of fusible web between the ribbon folds. Press and fuse the ribbon to the tie (D). You may want to use a press cloth to protect the fabric and the iron during this process.

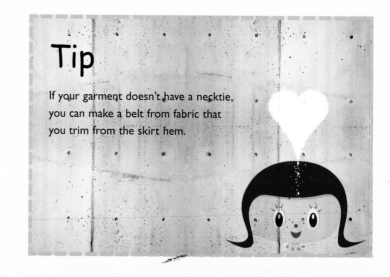

## Tip

If your garment doesn't have a necktie, you can make a belt from fabric that you trim from the skirt hem.

A

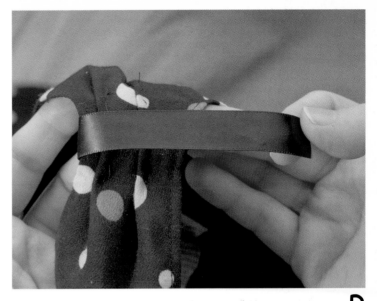

B

C

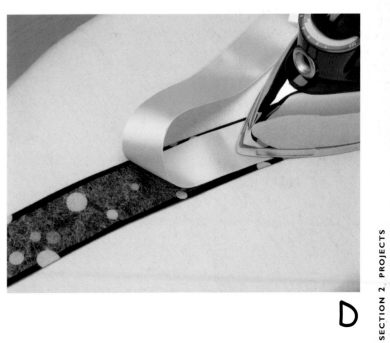

D

8. Machine stitch the ribbon to the tie, staying close to the ribbon edge (E). If the ribbon is a contrasting color, stitch with the ribbon color on the spool position and the dress color thread on the bobbin. Use a new machine needle while stitching, since a dull needle can make pulls in the satin.

9. Try on the dress and belt, and pin-mark locations for carriers above and below the belt. Make thread belt carriers (see page 28) at these positions.

10. The tulle makes this dress much longer, so you might want to shorten it. Your dress will probably have a slit at the center back hem, for ease in walking. If you shorten your dress, you can close this slit, or keep it open. Make the lining the same length—or a bit shorter—than the dress. If an adjustment is desired, do this now. Fuse a 2" (5.1 cm) -wide strip of interfacing to the wrong side of the lining hem to support the attached tulle.

11. The tulle used for this dress is sold folded. Fold the tulle again, so that you can cut four layers at a time.

12. Measure and cut fourteen panels, each 10" (25.4 cm) wide on the lengthwise grain, of each color, for a total of twenty-eight panels.

13. Adjust the sewing machine stitch length to 3 (9 spi) and loosen the top (needle thread) tension. Gather each panel with two rows of stitches along the crosswise grain of each panel. Sew the first row of stitching ¼" (6 mm) in from the edge. Sew the second row ¼" (6 mm) from the first row (F).

14. Pull the two bobbin threads to gather the tulle evenly. Join the same-color panels together, end-to-end along the 10" (25.4 cm) edge, with a ¼" (6 mm) seam allowance (F). In the same manner, make a gathered tulle strip with the second color.

15. Decide which color of tulle ruffle will be underneath. Overlap, and then stitch, the top of this ruffle on the wrong side of the lining, at the hem (G). Mark a chalk line 1" (2.5 cm) above the first ruffle. Pin and stitch the remaining ruffle to the lining. The ruffles are left open at the back slit. The lower half can be joined if desired.

16. Shorten the dress to a length that just covers the gathering seam allowance of the top ruffle. Make a new, 1½" (3.8 cm) -wide dress hem by turning the edge under or applying seam binding and hand stitching the hem (H). (See pages 14–15 for Hem techniques.)

17. Attach a permanent bow belt (see page 22).

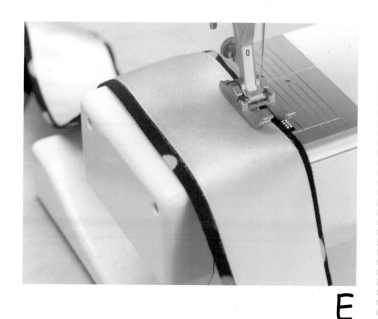

E

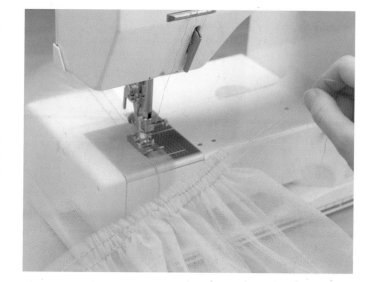

F

G

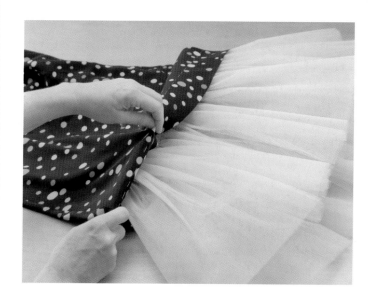

H

# WALL STREET TO CHIC SHEATH

The wool crepe fabric and simple styling of this dress initially proved attractive, and the flattering fit sealed the deal. A simple solution turns this serious, boxy look into a sleek, pencil-slim sheath. The horizontal seaming lends itself to the use of the sleeves to lengthen the skirt.

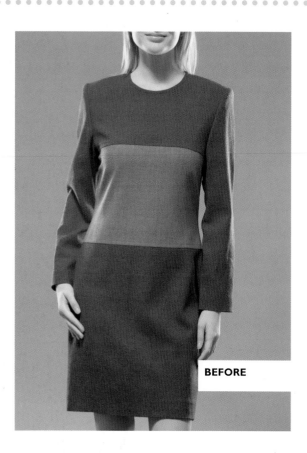

**BEFORE**

**LEVEL OF SKILL:** ★★

## materials

- basic sewing kit (see page 13)
- dress with long sleeves
- sewing thread, color-matched to the garment
- 1½ yards (1.4 m) of ½" (13 mm) -wide single-fold bias tape
- 1½ yards (1.4 m) of seam binding (optional)
- narrow belt

AFTER

## instructions

1. Release and pull the lining away from the bodice area of the dress. Remove the shoulder pads, sleeves, and sleeve linings (A). Stretch the seams apart when using a seam ripper for quick separation (B).

2. The armhole of this dress was beautifully tailored with interfacing and tape. With the shoulder pads gone, the armholes needs to be reshaped. Reduce the shoulder height by lowering the end of each shoulder (outermost edge, which was closest to the sleeve) ¼" (6 mm) and tapering the new seamline back to the original shoulder seamline at the neckline (C). Stitch the altered shoulder seam. Try on the dress, and pin-fit along both side seams. Take in at least ½" (1.3 cm) at the underarm and waist. Taper to the original seamline at the hip. Make sure that you adjust both side seams the same amount. Mark the alterations on the dress with chalk. Stitch the side seams of the dress and the lining separately.

3. For a scooped armhole, start reshaping by pinning twill tape around the armhole, beginning at the midpoint of the shoulder seam. Mark the armhole by pinning through the dress fabric and the lining. Curve the line down so that it drops 1" (2.5 cm) below the armhole (D). Balance the front and back marked lines so that they have the same shape. Hand baste the twill tape. Machine staystitch around the new armhole alongside the twill tape, sewing through the dress fabric and lining. Trim the seam allowance width to ¼" (6 mm) and remove the twill tape (D). To make the other armhole the exact same shape, use the trimmed seam allowance as a guide.

4. Open one long edge of the single-fold bias tape. With the right sides together, pin the tape around the new armhole, easing the edge around the curves. Stitch along the tape's fold line, clip, turn the tape to the inside of the dress along the seamline, and topstitch through all layers ⅜" (1 cm) from the edge (E).

5. Release the original hemline and steam-press the hem flat. Unless the crease completely disappears, use the fold line of the hem as the seamline for the new hem band that you're adding. Measure around the entire dress at the new seamline (F). Since the skirt has a center back kick pleat, this will require extra fabric for the underlay because the ends overlap. If you don't have enough fabric, you can piece the underlay with sleeve scraps. Repeat this process with the sleeve lining for the skirt lining.

6. Stitch the bands to the skirt hem. Piece the sleeves together by positioning the seams at the side seams on the dress. Press the seam allowances up and topstitch the seam exactly like the others, ⅜" (1 cm) from the seamline. Finish the hem edge with zigzag or overlock stitches or seam binding. Blind hem the hem allowance in place. (See page 14 for Basic Stitches.)

7. Attach the hem band lining (formerly the sleeve lining) to the bottom of the skirt lining in the same manner.

## Tips

A wide band of velvet, lace, or embroidery can lengthen any dress. Add a touch of the contrast fabric at the neckline or shoulder to unify the look. A cuffed or pieced effect can also add interest to a lengthened skirt. The longer and narrower the skirt, the longer the back slit for ease in walking.

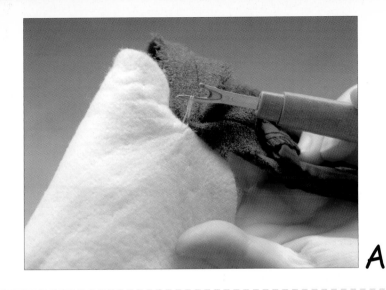

A

B

C

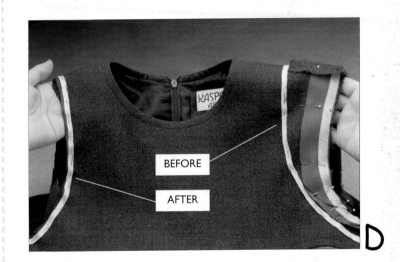

BEFORE

AFTER

D

E

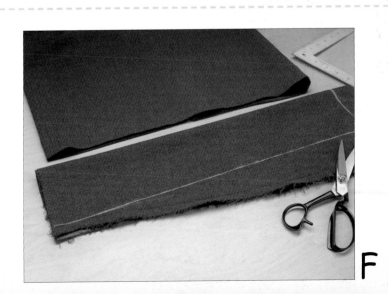

F

AFTER

# '60s MOD TO MOD MAIDEN

This boldly graphic polyester dress from the '60s had been sadly neglected. Its hem was down and the belt was missing.

A graceful neckline, three-quarter length sleeves, and a simple belt make it a hot commodity!

**BEFORE**

**LEVEL OF SKILL:** ★★★

## materials

- basic sewing kit (see page 13)
- unlined dress with a center back zipper and any type of collar attached to a high neckline
- 3 yards (2.7 m) of rayon seam binding
- ¼ yard (22.8 cm) of fusible tricot (knit) interfacing
- sewing thread, color-matched to the dress
- sewing thread, color-matched to the belt
- 1 yard (0.9 m) of ⅞" (22 mm) -wide single fold bias tape
- hook and eye (optional, see step 4)
- 1 yard (0.9 m) of 2" (5.1 cm) -wide stretch elastic, color-matched to the skirt motif, for the belt
- zipper presser foot
- belt buckle to fit the belt width

Note: The belt elastic will not be covered with fabric.

## instructions

1. Remove the collar from the neckline and the top of the zipper. Don't cut through the zipper. To create the bateau neckline style, pin-mark the center front of the neckline and the midpoint of both shoulder seams. Mark the style line by pinning twill tape across the front and back, keeping the original center front and center back levels the same. The line made by the twill tape will be slightly curved (A).

2. Thread-trace the new neckline along the tape line, making sure each side is exactly the same. Chalk in a ¼" (6 mm) seam allowance above the thread tracing and cut along that chalk line, trimming away the old neckline.

3. Lay the new neckline down on the interfacing, matching the center front and back to the straight grain of the interfacing. Pin and chalk-mark the new neckline edge and shoulder line onto the interfacing. Using the tracing line as one edge, mark and cut two strips of interfacing, each 1½" (3.8 cm) wide. Don't add seam allowances at the shoulder seams. Pin and fuse the interfacing onto the wrong side of the neckline, both front and back. The interfacing doesn't need to extend onto the zipper tape at center back.

4. For the front neckline facing, measure and cut a strip of bias tape the length of the front neckline plus 3" (7.6 cm). For the back facing, add 1½" (3.8 cm) to the back neck measurement. (The shoulder seam of the bias facing is angled, so you need extra to accommodate the shape.) Unfold a lengthwise edge of the bias tape. Center and pin the bias tape pieces on the neckline, with the right sides together. Let the short ends of the bias tape extend beyond the zipper. Stitch the tape to the neckline with a ¼" (6 mm) seam allowance. Leave the short ends of the bias tape seam allowances free at the shoulder/ neck points and backstitch the seamline at those points. Press the seam allowance toward the bias tape and understitch (see page 16).

5. Fold and slipstitch the front bias tape shoulder seam allowances over the raw edge of the back bias tape, and tack the outer edge of the bias tape in place on the dress shoulder seam (B). Fold both short ends of the bias tape under at center back and slipstitch the folds along the zipper. If you choose not to encase the top of the zipper inside the bias tape, make sure that the fold and slipstitches don't prevent the zipper tape from sliding. The top of the zipper may need to be adjusted and restitched. A hook and eye at the top is optional.

5. To create a three-quarter length sleeve, measure and chalk 3 ¾" (9.5 cm) above the sleeve hem. Try on the dress to double check the measurement, then cut along the chalked line. If the sleeve is laid flat with the underarm seam along one edge, the cut line should be perpendicular to the fold, which is the center grainline. Open the bottom 2" (5.1 cm) of the underarm seam, to create a slit for a slightly flared sleeve hem.

6. Mark the sleeve hem 1" (2.5 cm) up from the cut edge and thread-trace. If the original skirt hemline crease is faint, thread-trace it, as well. Machine staystitch the hem edges ¼" (6 mm) in from the cut edges.

7. Aligning one long edge with the staystitching, pin and machine stitch the seam binding to the right side of the sleeve and skirt hems (C). Along the thread tracings, fold up the sleeve hem allowance and hand stitch it in position with a slant stitch, picking up the tiniest amount of fabric with the needle as stitching. (See page 14 for Basic Stitches.)

8. Since there is little seam allowance around the sleeve hem split, cut two pieces of 3" (7.6 cm) -long pieces of seam binding. Stitch a length of seam binding on each side of the sleeve hem split, to create a facing. Tuck under ½" (1.3 cm) at the hemline. Fold and then hand stitch the sleeve slit facing in place on the wrong side of fabric.

9. Hand stitch the skirt hem with a slant stitch (D). (See the finished effect on page 15.)

10. On the belt elastic, chalk a straight, perpendicular line ½" (1.3 cm) in from the cut edge. Adjust the sewing machine to a 5 (wide) zigzag width and short, 0.5 mm (20 spi) stitch length. Zigzag ¼" (6 mm) away from the straight edge, starting and stopping with a backstitch. Trim the elastic end close to the zigzag stitch for a finished edge (E).

11. Loop the finished end of the elastic through the buckle. Fold 1½" (3.8 cm) of the belt end back on itself and pin the end to the belt. Use a zipper foot and straight stitch the end in place (F).

12. Try on the belt and buckle it up. Mark, and then cut off, the extra length, if necessary. Finish the belt end in the same way as the other end.

A

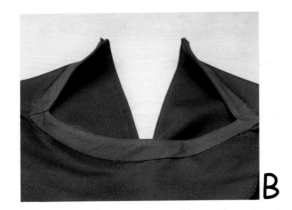

B

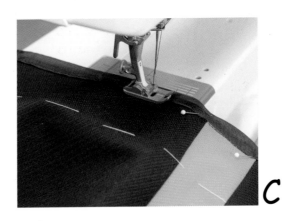

C

D

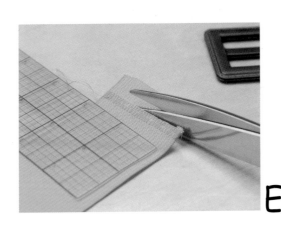

E

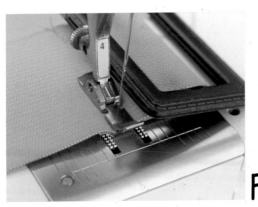

F

# WASHED-UP RAINCOAT TO CITY SLICKER

Deconstructed styles and raw edges are very current design details. This late-1980s raincoat had football sized shoulders and an unflattering length. The soft, wide lapel added to its bathrobe charm. By creating a new contrasting collar and shortening the skirt, the new proportions look great paired with a narrow skirt or slacks. The cutoff hem fabric is used to replace the missing belt. Custom covered buttons add a professional touch.

**BEFORE**

**LEVEL OF SKILL:** ★★★

## materials

- basic sewing kit (see page 13)
- raincoat with a notched shawl, or convertible collar (worn open with small lapels or closed at the neck without lapels, like a shirt collar)
- 1 yard (0.9 m) of contrasting fabric
- sewing thread, color-matched to the garment
- sewing thread, color-matched to the trim fabric
- 1½" × 3" (3.8 × 7.6 cm) of fusible web
- fabric-covered button kit for 6 buttons, each ⅞" (2.2 cm)
- ⅞" (2.2 cm) flat button for the inside
- 1½ yards (1.4 m) of 2" (5.1 cm) -wide belting
- 1 pair of 2" (5.1 cm) -wide D-rings
- zipper presser foot
- extra-fine silk pins
- fabric glue such as Fray Check

Note: If you want a narrow belt, 1¼" (32 mm) -wide belting is available, or use several layers of heavyweight interfacing rather than belting.

AFTER

## instructions

1. Remove the shoulder pads. They can be replaced with a new pair that isn't as thick, if necessary.

2. If the coat's undercollar doesn't have a center back seam, fold the collar in half to find and pin-mark the center back. Pin-mark the roll line of the lapel, as well. Raincoat fabric is usually tightly woven and in some cases, rubberized. Use extra-fine silk pins for easier pinning and to prevent visible holes in the fabric.

3. Spread the contrasting fabric flat, on the fold, on a cutting surface. If a dominant pattern such as a stripe or plaid is used, match the pattern at the selvage and cut the ends. Mark a bias line diagonally (at a 45-degree angle to the grain of the fabric) with chalk close to one end of the yardage. A quick way to determine true bias is to fold the selvage edge (lengthwise grain) back on the fabric, lining it up with the crosswise grain to form a triangle. The fold is the bias. Cutting woven fabric on the bias minimizes fraying.

4. Pin the right center front of the coat facedown on the bias line marked on the fabric. Smooth and flatten the lapel and half the collar (from the front opening to the center back line) on the fabric. Pin and chalk-mark the center back line of the collar on the fabric. Pin the coat to the fabric along the neckline of the collar, stopping 2" (5.1 cm) before the collar/lapel notch at the center front (A). Pin along the roll line of the lapel, which ends at the top buttonhole. Pin the outer edges of the collar and lapel to 4" (10.2 cm) below the buttonhole at the center front. When finished, the lapel overlay will run alongside—but not cover—the buttonhole.

5. With chalk, add a ½" (1.3 cm) seam allowance to the center back collar, outer lapel, and collar edge. Extend the lapel and collar seam allowance lines ½" (1.3 cm) to create points on

the rounded corners. Pull the coat back and mark the neckline and the roll line of the lapel. Add a 1" (2.5 cm) seam allowance to the neckline and 2" (5.1 cm) to the roll line. These seam allowances can be clipped and trimmed later, after the contrasting fabric piece is fitted to the coat.

6. Cut out the lapel/collar facing that you traced on the fabric in the previous steps. To reinforce the extended collar and lapel points, cut out triangles of fusible web and fabric and fuse these to the underside of the points (B).

7. For topstitching, use thread that's matched to the coat in the needle and thread matched to the contrasting fabric in the bobbin. Since the collar overlay (the contrasting fabric) is stitched from the underside, balance the machine tension so the bobbin thread looks as good as the top.

8. Match the stripe or print of the collar overlay together at the center back neck (C).

9. Machine stitch the center back collar seam and press the seam allowances open. Place the wrong side of the facing on top of the coat collar and lapel. Pin the layers together, placing the pins perpendicular to the neckline seam and down the roll line.

10. From the coat side, machine stitch along the neckline (D). Hand baste along the roll line, ending at the center front

*continued on page 112*

# Tip

If there are belt carriers on your coat, make the finished width of the belt to fit through them. If you want a superwide belt, just make your own thread belt carriers (see page 26).

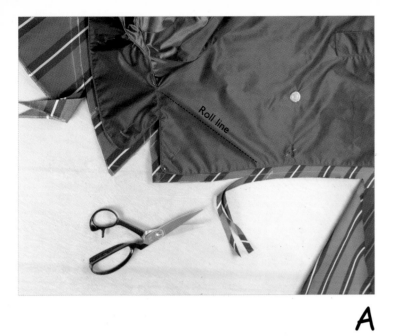

**A**

**B**

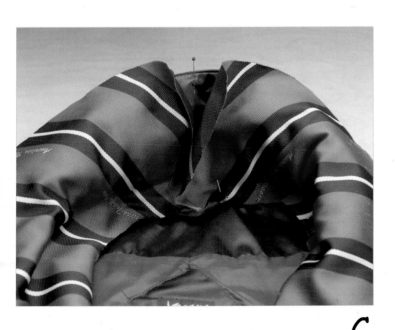

**C**

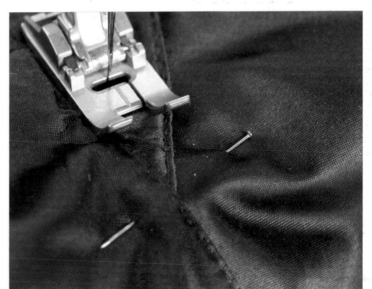

**D**

about 2" (5.1 cm) below the buttonhole (E). Try the coat on to check the roll of the collar. Machine stitch ¾" (1.9 cm) in (toward the body of the coat) from the roll line connecting to the neckline stitching and down to below the buttonhole. Trim close to the stitching line.

11. Smooth and pin the overlay out to the edges, curving the fabric layers over your hand to maintain the collar and lapel roll (F). Pin and stitch close to the collar and lapel edges. Use a zipper foot for accuracy. From the underside, trim the seam allowance along the coat edge (G). At the extended collar and lapel points, trim close to the stitching. Fabric glue such as Fray Check can be used on cut edges that you think will fray excessively.

12. Mark the new coat length at 1½" (3.8 cm) below the bottom of the pocket bag. Add 1½" (3.8 cm) for the hem allowance. At the bottom of the coat, release the lining where it is joined to the facing. Later, the lining will be hemmed separately. Keep the lining 1" (2.5 cm) shorter than the coat. Cut off the coat's original hem and reserve it for the belt (H).

13. Pick out 3" (7.6 cm) of topstitching on the lower edge of the center front along the facing edge. Turn the facing back on itself (so the facing is on the outside of the coat) and machine stitch along the new hemline (the line you made at the start of step 12). Trim the facing seam allowance down to ¼" (6 mm). Turn the facing back inside and hand stitch the loose, released vertical edge of the facing to the lining. Press or baste under the cut edge of the coat hem ½" (1.3 cm). Turn the hem again 1" (2.5 cm) and machine stitch in place.

14. The width of the belt is determined by the width of the existing belt carriers. The finished length is your waist measurement plus 2" (5.1 cm) of ease (see page 128) and 1½" (3.8 cm) for the turn-back for the D-rings plus 12" (30.5 cm) for the belt extension. Cut the belting to this measurement.

15. Cut clean, perpendicular ends across the belting. To create a point on the extension end, draw diagonal lines from the midpoint of the belting width and cut. Use a seam ripper to open the original hem of the coat to provide a seam allowance for the belt. Encase the belting with the fabric and pin the fabric edge together with the seamline close to one edge of the belt. The coat's original hemline becomes one of the lengthwise edges of the belt. Mark the pointed belt end on the fabric, add a ¼" (6 mm) seam allowance and trim off the excess fabric. Turn under the seam allowances, pin the edges together snugly and slipstitch the fabric cover over the belting (I). Topstitch around the belt close to the edges. Attach the D-rings through the straight belt end and turn the end under to form a facing. Use a zipper foot to stitch as close to the rings as possible, through all layers.

16. Use a kit to cover the buttons with fabric. Make a small running stitch around the edge of each fabric circle (J). Place the button top in the center and pull the thread so that the fabric gathers up evenly over the button. Complete each button by following the kit instructions. Remove any remaining original buttons from the coat and stitch the new ones in place. For a double-breasted coat, stitch a flat button inside the underlay.

# Tips

- Work with, rather than avoid, quirky fabric. The contrasting fabric shown in the photos for this project was found in a fabric store that was going out of business. Apparently it is men's tie fabric that has American Family Insurance written on it. Imagine all the male employees of a company wearing one.

- The contrasting fabric overlay can be cut in two pieces (collar and lapel), with a raw edged neck seam extending out to the notch. A frayed trim or edging can be added to emphasize this design detail.

- To avoid globbing too much glue along a cut edge, dip a toothpick in the glue and run this along the edge.

E

F

G

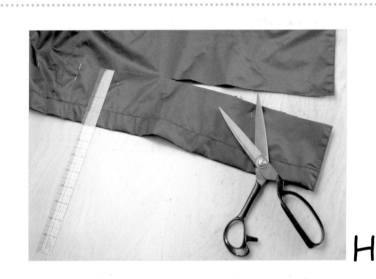

H

I

J

AFTER

# DRAB KHAKI TO DELICATE DETAILING

The fancy tablecloth was hopelessly stained but the Battenberg lace insets were worthy of a transplant. A simple skirt is the perfect recipient. From the late '50s, this skirt had a 23" (58.4 cm) waist, which needed to be expanded. The added ribbon and lace detailing are like frosting on a cake.

**BEFORE**

## LEVEL OF SKILL: ★

### materials

- basic sewing kit (see page 13)
- skirt (flare dirndl, A-line, or straight)
- Battenberg lace tablecloth or motifs
- sewing thread, color-matched to the garment
- sewing thread, color-matched to the lace
- 2 yards (1.8 m) of 1" (25 mm) -wide grosgrain ribbon
- hook-and-eye set
- large piece of cardboard

Note: The grosgrain ribbon needs to be twice your waist measurement plus ease and extension (which varies on skirts). Two yards (1.8 m) should be plenty, but it's a good idea to check your waist measurement; do the math and be sure.

## instructions

1. Choose Battenberg lace motifs on the cloth that are best suited to border the hem of the skirt. Additional motifs can embellish other parts of the skirt. Cut out the selected motifs, leaving a margin of fabric around each one. Where dominant motifs connect, carefully separate them by cutting along an outer edge of a tape or embroidered line. Arrange the lace pieces on the skirt with scalloped edges extending past the hemline (A). If you place motifs on the upper skirt, try on the garment to make sure that you like their positions.

2. Remove the waistband of the skirt with a seam ripper (B).

3. Slide a large piece of cardboard between the front and back skirt to create a surface on which to pin the lace in place on the skirt. Trim the fabric away from the lace parts that overlap at the hem. Join the lace using small, even hand stitches (C).

4. Pin inside the motifs, away from the edges of the lace (D).

5. Hand stitch close to the edges of the lace, through all layers, using small, even running stitches (E).

6. The wrong side of the garment will resemble a hand-stitched quilt (F).

7. When the sewing is complete, trim all remaining fabric away from the lace edges with a pair of small, sharp embroidery scissors (G).

8. Stretch and smooth out any ease stitches around the waist seam, to enlarge the waist. Pin the grosgrain ribbon to the right side of the skirt, slightly below the original waist seam-line. At the opening, allow for a 1" (2.5 cm) extension at one end, for a hook-and-eye closure. At the end of the extension, fold the ribbon back on itself (across the width) and pin the long edge inside the waistband (H). Don't fold the ribbon lengthwise. You are sandwiching the waist seam allowance between two strips of ribbon. Match the top edges of the ribbons. Machine edgestitch the ribbons along the waist, ends, and top. Finish with a hook and eye set at the opening on the new grosgrain waistband. A detachable bow can be pinned at the waist.

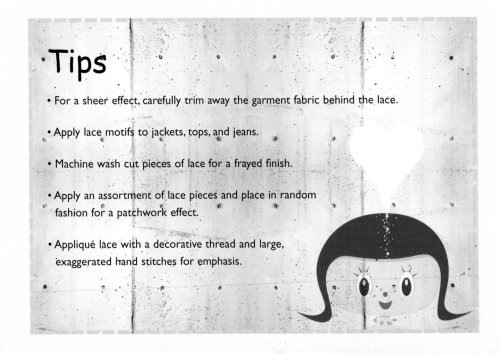

## Tips

• For a sheer effect, carefully trim away the garment fabric behind the lace.

• Apply lace motifs to jackets, tops, and jeans.

• Machine wash cut pieces of lace for a frayed finish.

• Apply an assortment of lace pieces and place in random fashion for a patchwork effect.

• Appliqué lace with a decorative thread and large, exaggerated hand stitches for emphasis.

A

B

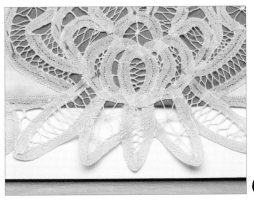

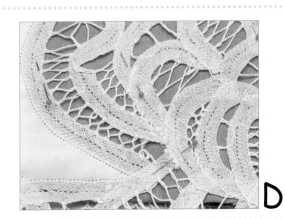

C

D

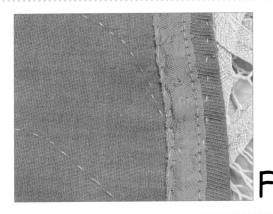

E

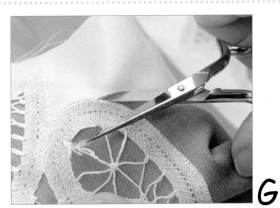

F

G

H

# technique boutique

**Resourceful** is the term that best describes the guest contributors who delivered a **witty** collection of modified clothing and accessories. Working independently from each other, they crafted pieces whose themes were remarkably intertwined. The **menswear influence** is strong as is the **Victorian** look and use of unique prints. Most of the pieces were completed on a shoestring. My students made six of the projects and the others are done by recent college graduates, save one. I hope you are inspired by **"shopping" the techniques** highlighted in each of the projects.

3

**AFTER**

# Mismatched Prints
# to Mixed-up Print Dress
**Designer: Sharon Sued Chavez**

Vintage prints, large and small, are what get this designer's attention. Her shopping trip to a local thrift store yielded a camisole top and a men's tie. The spicy combination of pattern and color produces a delicious summer dress.

- Cut two lengths of a complementary print purchased at a fabric store.

- Stitch side seams.

- Hand tuck the waist.

- Join the skirt to the waistline of the top.

- Insert a zipper on the side.

BEFORE

BEFORE

BEFORE

AFTER

AFTER

AFTER

# Oxford Shirt to Flirty Minidress

**Designer: Jamie Davis Gaul**

Deconstruct dad's classic button-down shirt and a kicky minidress emerges. Choose a shirt long enough to reach mid-thigh.

- Remove the sleeves.
- Take in the side seams down to the hip level.
- Create inverted pleats on the sides.
- Cut off the upper portion of the sleeves for a three-quarter length.
- Rotate and reattach the cut-off sleeves, bringing the placket details forward.
- Create epaulettes from the pocket.
- Trim with vintage military buttons and scarf sash.

# Safari-Style to Victorian Flair

**Designer: Roberto Calasanz Mendez**

This linen jacket was given to the designer in the early '90s, but he never wore it.

Inspired by the books, *Images of America: Caribbean Americans in New York City 1895–1975* and *Dress in Detail from Around the World*, he decided to transform this boxy, baggy piece into a shapely, hourglass silhouette.

- Wash jacket with fabric softener.
- Tea dye jacket.
- Replace buttons.
- Cover the collar and pocket flaps with Venice lace.
- Pleat the shoulders.
- Pin tuck the back waist and sleeve cuffs.
- Add adjustable tabs to the waist for shaping.

# Designer Vintage to Victorian with a Twist

**Designer: Sharon Seo**

A Betsey Johnson dress, worn to the ninth grade homecoming dance, hung in the closet unworn for ten years. Its owner decided to turn the dress into a Victorian-style blouse. Now this versatile top dresses up any skirt or jean with panache.

- Cut off the skirt of the dress and slip.
- Insert elastic through the new hemline.
- Create capelet sleeves by gathering and stitching portions of the skirt to the armholes.
- Make a lace scarf with the leftover fabric (not shown).

**AFTER**

## Western-Style Denim Shirt to a Cropped, Flared Jacket

**Designer: Olivia Plyer**

Ever heard the expression, "He'd give you the shirt off his back"? That's precisely how this designer, who loves to play with volume and proportion, obtained a garment to renovate. The results yield an ideal marriage of men's styling and woman's fancy.

- Cut off the front of the shirt below the pockets.

- Scoop out the back of the shirt below the yoke.

- Replace the back with the gathered cutoff front.

- Remove the sleeves.

- Take in the body to reduce the width.

- Raise the armholes.

- Shape, gather, switch, and set back in the lower third of the sleeves.

# Dated Miniskirt to Flashy Strapless Dress

**Designer: Sarah Chang**

Is there a high school miniskirt in your closet in need of revamping? This little number is suitable for all the "hot spots" in town.

- Hike up skirt under the arms.
- Add darts below the bust for a fitted, strapless bodice.
- Attach a skirt of dyed silk to the bodice.
- Cover the high waistline with a belt, such as the whimsical '70s one shown.

# Boho Bandana to Sassy Tank

**Designer: Vivienne Mok**

The "hippie/pirate" look was the rage when this designer was a fifteen-year-old high school student. Hooked on wearing head scarves, she collected bandanas wherever she traveled, and found this one in Hong Kong. A few quick snips and she's got the perfect summer top.

- Turn the bandana on the bias and trim and hem it to fit the front of the bodice.
- Stitch a rectangle of contrasting fabric to the back, and create one thin strap from a strip of this fabric. Create the second strap from the trimmed bandana border.
- Attach the straps to the bodice, crisscrossing them in the back.
- Place a separating zipper on the side, and embellish the print with crystal rhinestones, radiating from the center.

# Simple Tee to Ruffles Galore

**Designer: Sarah Chang**

Turn a tiny tee into a precious commodity by trading a classic ribbed V-neck for a flourish of frills and sparkle.

- Clip the neckband and turn it under.
- Stitch on satin ruffles and sequined trim.
- Embellish with a mix of beads, buttons, and charms.

**AFTER**

**BEFORE**

## Frosted Denim to Frilly Handbag
**Designer: Vivienne Mok**

Can't bear to part with an old pair of jeans or skirt that doesn't fit anymore? Convert it into a bag so it can enjo second wind. This one is fully lined and zips at the top.

- Remove the legs (and crotch) and sew the edges together from the inside.

- Sew handles from the excess fabric.

- Adorn the bag with white fabric paint, suede fring crystal rhinestones, metal studs, frayed and ruffled denim, and lace.

BEFORE

BEFORE

BEFORE

AFTER

AFTER

AFTER

# Oversized Cuffed Shirt to Lacey Tunic

**Designer: Cham Sum Chan**

The relationship was over. A few of his things were left hanging in her closet. What was she to do with them? An ex-boyfriend's shirt morphs into a femininely fashioned chemise. If only he could see her now.

- Remove the sleeves.
- Gather the fabric across the back of the shirt.
- Cover the yoke and gathering line with Chantilly lace.
- Stitch elastic around the waist, and wrap it with a velvet ribbon.

# Bland Belt to South Pacific Hip

**Designer: Camille Mun**

Purchased at a department store, this belt's buckle featured the name of a popular Korean design house, which has since gone out of business. A bit of fluff and flourish and your jeans will never look the same!

- Hot-glue a beaded cord down the center of the belt.
- Place handmade fabric rosettes and metallic embellishments along the cord.
- Snap off the old buckle and replace it with a new one.

# Downtrodden Heels to Twinkle Toes

**Designer: Michelle Boyce**

Worn by models in a designer's showroom, these Italian-made heels were comfortable but had become dingy from wear. What better reason does a girl need other than "new" shoes to get out and celebrate?

- Paint the shoes.
- Attach sparkly trim as heel straps.
- Tuck feathers beneath the trim.

# patterns

## ROSEBUD

(see page 26)

Pattern shown at actual size

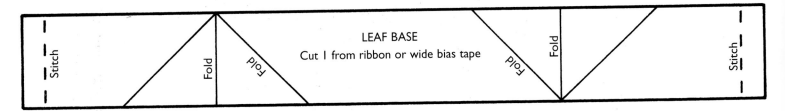

Stitch | Fold | Fold | LEAF BASE — Cut I from ribbon or wide bias tape | Fold | Fold | Stitch

## PLAIN-JANE JACKET TO KNIT AND NYLON EYE-CATCHER

(see page 86)

Photocopy at 200%

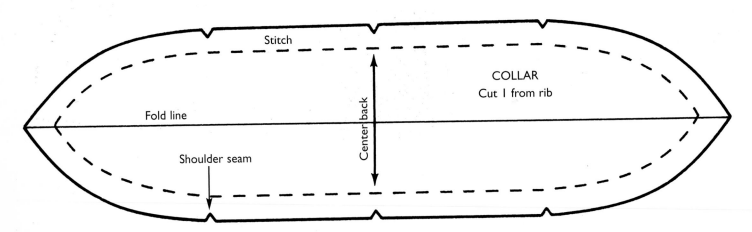

Stitch

Fold line

Shoulder seam

Center back

COLLAR
Cut I from rib

# POCKETED TOTE

(see page 50)

Photocopy at 125%

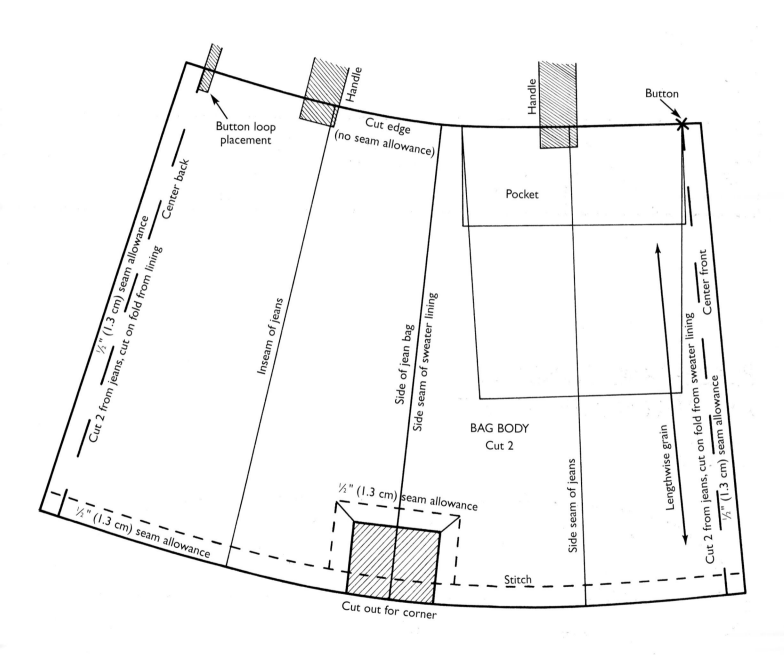

Button loop placement

Handle

Cut edge (no seam allowance)

Handle

Button

Pocket

Center back

½" (1.3 cm) seam allowance

Cut 2 from jeans, cut on fold from lining

Inseam of jeans

Side of jean bag

Side seam of sweater lining

BAG BODY
Cut 2

Lengthwise grain

Side seam of jeans

Center front

Cut 2 from jeans, cut on fold from sweater lining

½" (1.3 cm) seam allowance

½" (1.3 cm) seam allowance

½" (1.3 cm) seam allowance

Stitch

Cut out for corner

# POCKETED TOTE continued

Photocopy at 145%

| |
|---|
| Place on fold — HANDLE     Cut 2 from pant leg hem     Cut 2 from ribbon     ⁷⁄₈" (2.2 cm) |

$\tfrac{7}{8}$" (2.2 cm)

← 22" (55.9 cm) →

Photocopy at 100%

BUTTON LOOP     Cut 1 from jeans

Fold